**Brighton & Hove
City Council**

BRIGHTON & HOVE CITY LIBRARIES

Jubilee Library

Jubilee Street, Brighton BN1 1GE
Tel: 01273 290800

Wh   :ter
our: all
that

My message is about the possibility of the ultimate betterment
of a human being—not of mankind, not of a country, not of
a social belief, but of a human being. And it is not through
ideas or concepts. Neither is it through hearsay or repetition.

It is through each individual exploring and finding the beauty
within themselves.

—Prem Rawat

03398599

Adi means *ancient* ancient: being old in wisdom and experience; dating from a remote period; of great age; having the qualities associated with age, wisdom, or long use; venerable.

PREM RAWAT
SPOKEN WORDS

The Greatest Truth of All:
You Are Alive

an ADI book

For information, address Words of Peace Global, P.O. Box 2745, CS Amsterdam, The Netherlands.

ISBN: 978-1481028875

EDITOR: Ole Grünbaum
COVER DESIGN: Giorgio Menzio
PAGE LAYOUT: Peter Petrovich
ORIGINAL ADI DESIGN: Rasmus Olesen
COVER PHOTOS: Mary Rozzi
AUDIENCE PHOTOS: Carla Cahill, Gustavo Ten-Hoever, Jaques Masraff, Marie-Catherine Toulet, Mehau Kulyk
EDITORIAL STAFF: Mary Wishard, Sherry Weinstein, Sara Shaffer, Jan Buchalter, Lynne Laffe, Pegi Hope Cohen

Prem Rawat, also known as Maharaji, delivers his message of peace to many diverse audiences around the world. This compilation, *The Greatest Truth of All: You Are Alive,* was derived from his talks and edited for brevity and ease of reading. The audience photographs were taken at Prem Rawat's events, though not necessarily those featured in this publication.

The Greatest Truth of All: You Are Alive can be ordered on the following websites:

www.store.wopg.org
www.amazon.com

CONTENTS

PART FOUR: YOUR HOME OF EXISTENCE

INTRODUCTION

Born in 1957, Prem Rawat began speaking publicly about peace at an early age. He has traveled internationally for more than four decades, speaking to people from every background and culture—from villagers to national leaders, from prisoners to corporate executives. He speaks extemporarily from his heart, engaging audiences with humor, clarity and warmth.

In his own words:

"It is my privilege, my joy, my honor, to go around the world and tell people about the possibility of being in peace.

It is a message of the heart. I don't prepare my speeches. I come, I open my heart and, with a sense of clarity, a sense of understanding, and hopefully with humility, I present what I have to say."

His words are living words to live audiences: words not only about peace, but words that have the capacity to evoke the feeling of peace, a personal peace within each person. Many people have commented that when they heard him speak, even though it was to a large gathering, it was as if he spoke to them individually.

This collection of twenty-one edited talks is compiled in the hope that the reader may not only sense the voice that spoke these words, but also engage in the most intriguing conversation of all time, arising from very simple questions like "Why am I alive?" and "What is possible in a human life?"

This book is not a work of suspense that one needs to read page by page until the end finally reveals the answer to the riddle. The stories can be read in any order. Right from the beginning pages Prem Rawat makes clear that the answers are not to be found in thought and logic, or in words, but only in a feeling, and that this feeling is never far from anyone.

In my own experience, the feeling of peace that Prem Rawat speaks about is the most exquisite of all, and at the same time the most needed ingredient to make sense of life and to live happily.

The Editor

PS. There are many opportunities available to hear Prem Rawat speak, either through live events, television programs or online videos and audio clips. See www.wopg.org.

The words alone are quite nice,
but it's not about the words.

It's about breaking through the wall of words
—into reality.

If I could see that it is not
the complicated, but the simple within me
—not the scales, not the weights,
but an ocean of joy
—then I would realize:

This is who I am.
Simple. Beautiful. And with one thirst.
To be content. To be in peace.
To be in joy. To understand.

PART ONE

WHO AM I?

THE REALITY OF EXISTENCE

I talk about something very simple. Of course, people hope that they will hear something they haven't heard before, because somehow we have equated "new" and "different" with "exciting." But new and different have nothing to do with exciting. Exciting is exciting. It could be new, it could be old, it could be different, or it could be very familiar, and that wouldn't make any difference, because the excitement has to come from the inside.

I have been talking to people for four decades, and that's a long time. I started very young. I've traveled the world, and I've spoken to a lot of people in different places in their lives, from incredible sadness to incredible joy. From having the idea that "Everything is fine; I don't need anything more," to, "I have nothing." The variety and the space and the spectrum has been incredible.

MANY REALITIES

For me, there are perhaps many realities that manifest during a day. If bad news comes, that's a reality. If I have responsibilities to take care of, that's a reality. But I also know that for all the realities that are ever-changing, there is one reality that always remains exactly the same. And that reality addresses *me*.

We get very confronted by these realities. We're prepared for so many things in our lives, but when a new one comes, it is totally unexpected. It drops in our lap like somebody is saying, "Handle this!" Because we're unprepared, we say, "Whoa. How am I going to take care of that?"

I remember so clearly this lady I passed on the freeway when I was in Boston. She was going off for the weekend in her SUV with skateboards and bicycles and coolers, as though she was going to have a party. Somehow the bicycle fell off, and there was a police officer standing there, looking at her as she was trying to put it back on the car. You didn't even have to see it. As you drove by her, you could feel the frustration.

WHO AM I?

I know how you look at yourself. You look at yourself in a totally different way than you actually are. This is not nice. It's okay, but it's not nice. Who am I? If I see one of my kids in front of me, I become a father. "Everything okay? How are you doing? What's up? Where are you going? When are you going to be back?" There is that part of me, and I become that. Then I walk into my office and I've got all this paperwork and things to do, and I become that. But who am I, really? People call me by a name. I associate that name with myself. But who am I? What am I? Am I the complicated one that I see? Is this life of mine really as complicated as I have made it?

All that I weigh and measure my life with, the good and the bad, is that really me? The person who's going through a crisis, the person who's going through a vacation, the person who's going through this, and the person who's going through that? Or am I something else?

What am I? If I could see that it is not the complicated, but it is indeed the simple that is within me—not the scales, not the weights, but an ocean of joy—then I would realize this is who I am. Simple. Beautiful. And with one simple thirst. The thirst to be content. The thirst to be in peace. The thirst to be in joy. The thirst to understand. I've become very good at questioning, and I question everything. But my ability to question has not diminished my ability to understand, and I want to understand, not just keep questioning. I want answers, not just questions. How does that work? I'll give you an analogy. A car is broken; all the rods are blown, and the pistons have big holes in them. The cam is broken, and the timing chain is destroyed. This engine is *not* going to start. So somebody brilliant comes along and says, "Aha. We can see that there is a problem here. The problem is that the car is rusted, the paint is peeling, the windows are shot, the tires are flat. So, let's help you fix this car. Let's repaint it."

Now this machine looks good. New windows, new polished chrome, new paint job. Nice brand-new tires. The car has been brought into incredible shape, and you say, "Oh, thank you very much for fixing it all up! Thanks!" But you still have a problem, don't you? It won't run. Before, you had an ugly car that didn't run. Now you have a beautiful car that still doesn't run. Why did you want the car in the first place? To be beautiful or ugly, or to go somewhere, which will obviously require that it runs?

What is the point of this analogy? The point is, everything we do, we do to be happy. We want to be happy. This includes going to the moon. It includes sending out signals to extraterrestrials, digging for oil—all the things we do.

We have many excuses for the things that we do, and fundamentally at the bottom of all these excuses is that if somehow, more joy could come our way, that would be very nice.

You hear a lot of things. You hear, "Good days come, bad days come." I use that. I call it "ups and downs." But there is a place inside of you that is neither up nor down. There's a place inside of you that is steady. There is the beautiful miracle, the beautiful symphony of existence taking place.

Peace is within you. The thirst for peace is within you. Good news! What does it mean? It means you don't have to go search for it. So many people used to come to me—and still do—and say, "I'm searching." And, of course, I say, "What are you searching for?" If you really are searching for peace, you won't find it. Why? Because you already have it. How do you find something you already have? How do you find something you never lost? How do you find something that has been tailing you every day of your life? It lies in the realm where breath comes and goes and brings the gift of existence to you. This, my friends, is the miracle of miracles.

THE TRUE MIRACLE
I was born in India, and in India, they have just as much a love affair with miracles as anywhere else. But what is the definition of a *miracle*? If milk starts to flow from a rock, that is a miracle. That boggles me. People don't consider it to be a miracle that a cow eats green grass and gives white milk. But if milk comes out of a rock, it's a miracle.

It's a fluke! And would you drink it? I wouldn't. If I'm driving along and suddenly

14

milk starts to come out from the middle of the steering wheel, I will pull over. I'm not going to say, "Wow. A miracle!" and drink that milk.

We have a fascination with miracles, but we don't understand what a real miracle is because when it happens right under our noses, we don't know about it. The fact that you exist is a miracle. It is the grandest of all miracles. You exist. *You*. You are alive. You can feel. You can feel pain, but more importantly, you can feel joy. You can feel turmoil, but most importantly, you can feel peace. Think about it. You can feel peace. You have the ability to feel contentment. It is no accident that time after time, those people who have felt this have forwarded the message on very clearly: "What you are looking for is within you."

Thousands of years ago, Socrates made a little comment: "Know thyself." Nowadays it has become a question: "What do you think he meant by, 'Know thyself'?" He didn't say, "What do you think it means to know thyself?" He could have said, "What do you think would happen if you knew yourself?" He didn't say that, either. He didn't say, "Do you think it would be important if you knew thyself?" He simply said, "Know thyself."

You ask the leaders, "Do you know where you are going?" They say, "Of course we know where we're going. Look at all these people behind us."

Know yourself. Know what you are. This beautiful symphony that you are. This beautiful seed that you are. This beautiful poetry that you are. This beautiful story that you are. This beautiful drama that you are. Know this drama. Know this poetry. Know this song. Know this symphony.

CHANGE THE FILM

Knowing that which is within you in itself brings joy, brings peace. Of course, people have definitions of what peace is. People look at the world and say, "Stop the wars; that's peace." My analogy for that is the world you see out there is just a bunch of screens. Who's the projector? The world leaders? It really is a peculiar situation. It's a bit like this: There's a whole bunch of people walking along. First, one person was walking on the road. And why was he walking? He was walking because he didn't know where he was going, but he wanted to find out where to go, so he was walking. The second person saw him walking on the road, so he got behind him. The third person saw two of them walking on the road, so that person got behind them. Pretty soon, you have a huge crowd. And who are the leaders in the very front? Do these people know where they're going? It depends who you ask. If you ask the people in the back, they will say, "Yes, of course we know where we are going, because the leaders in the front are taking us there." And if you ask the leaders, "Do you know where you are going?" they'll say, "Of course we know where we're going. Look at all these people behind us." Neither has anything to do with whether anybody really knows where they're going.

I know there are people who get very upset with this. If you do, go read history. It's documented. That's exactly what happens time after time. Has the time not come that we should stand on our own feet for peace? If you do not like what you see on the screen, don't blame the screen. Don't clean the screen. Don't polish the screen. It will only reflect what is being projected on it much better. If you do not like what you see on the screen, change the film, not the projector. This is a very important point, because this is exactly what is happening in the world. People are saying to themselves and are also being told, "You're no good; let's improve you. Let's change the projector. Let's tweak the projector."

Change the film. That is what is important. The miracle, the peace, the most beautiful film is waiting to be threaded onto this projector so that it can be shown. And it is not a story of desperation, trauma, drama, and what is lacking in the world. A lot of people look at what is lacking. Next time you see a forest, ask yourself, "What is that forest about?" It is about the seed that germinated, not the seed that did not germinate. No forest carries a little sign that says, "Here lies the seed that didn't come along." That's history. Life is about the seeds that germinated. You are about what works, not what doesn't work. Learn to measure this existence with what you have, not with what you *don't* have.

THE HEART SAYS GO FORWARD

You will begin to see that what you have is so much more powerful, so much more beautiful than what you don't have. Dreams are fulfilled. There is a peace dancing that is more beautiful, more tranquil, than you could have ever imagined. This is all inside of you. People say, "I'm too far away from all this." Too far away from that? One day you will be, that is true, but not right now. I'm not here to talk about what will happen to you after you die. Sorry. There are other ones who can tell you about that.

Fortunately, in this life, there is something called the *heart*, and it nudges you—not to back up but to go forward. So many of us would stand at the pinnacles of our life and do nothing but look back. And the heart says, "No. Turn around and go forward." Follow the river of time. Don't oppose it; move with it. Learn to flow with it.

16

Do you want to know the definition of success? Look at yourself. You are the success.

It'll take you places. Places you have never been. Places that are simple. Places that you need to be familiar with. Go. Go with certainty.

A lot of people say to me, "How do you know you can give me peace?" Here's an analogy: Imagine you're going somewhere. You're in a new town, and you get lost. Of course, the first thing you do is resist acknowledging that you're lost. So you keep driving, hoping that you will come across something familiar in the instructions and everything will be okay. But that doesn't happen. All that happens is you get more and more lost. Finally, sanity kicks in, and you say, "Okay, I'm going to ask for directions." But this is how you go about it (and this is the cute part): You roll down your window and say, "Excuse me, sir. Do you know where such-and-such street is?" The man says, "Yeah. Just go down two blocks and make a right." And you say, "Okay, thank you," roll up your window, and off you go. How do you know this man knows where that street is? Maybe he is standing there waiting for somebody to give *him* directions, and yet you feel certain?

What we should question, we don't, and what we should not question, we do. But even if we question the things we shouldn't question, we will get an answer when we ask the right question.

Is it possible to turn confusion into clarity? Yes. Is it possible to turn the complicated into the simple? Yes. Is it possible to remove the darkness and replace it with light? Yes. Is it possible to have peace in this life? Yes. It is possible. And now.

GET IT?

Peace is within you. This is what some people do. They say, "How do I get it?" I say, "Get what? Get it?" How can you get it? You've already got it. Get it? If you think you have to get it when you've already got it, you don't get it. And if you really want to get it, then understand that you have got it. Get it?

Everything in this life has been away from me, so I had to go get it. Everything in this life that I call an accomplishment, I had to go and get, whether it was a diploma, a certificate, a license—whatever. Our whole life has been get it, get it, get it. Then, all of a sudden, somebody comes along and says, "Oh, by the way, that which you really want to get, you got."

This is not like instant rice, where you get a container, throw it in the microwave, punch a few buttons, and you have "instant rice."

We used to have a farm where I grew up in India, and we grew our own basmati rice. When the rice cooked in our home, you could smell it four blocks away, and it smelled good. Instant rice? You may as well eat your sock. You may actually feel full for a longer period of time, and it may be more nutritious and definitely low carb,

18

and it is entirely possible it may actually have more flavor than instant rice. Who knows? It depends how long you've been wearing it.

We live in an instant world where we want everything now. But when it comes to something that you have always had in your life, there is no "instant."

Do you want to hear the whisper? And why is it a whisper? Because it has been left so far back. Turn down the volume. Something is whispering. Let it come. Beckon it to come closer and closer to you. Then, this voice, this whisper, this desire, this wish for peace and contentment will not be ignored but heard. That is the preparation you need to make. That is the simplest of things you need to do. I'm not talking about that weird voice of the great complicator that complicates everything. First, it leads you to fall in love with that thing in the window up until the point you buy it. After that, the climax just makes a ninety-degree turn and a forty-degree nosedive until you get it home and you have lost all interest in it. Then it goes in the great closet.

Peace is within you. The thirst for peace is within you. Good news! You don't have to go search for it.

People love closet space because they know they're going to buy these things when the great complicator comes along and says, "Buy that. You *need* that."

You walk in, the price is high. "Oh, I'll think about it, okay?" Yes, you will. You will think, "I need that. I want it. I need to buy myself a treat; I haven't bought anything for myself for so long. It'll be a present, an early birthday present for myself." Excuses—a dime a dozen. And then, okay, you go and put it on the credit card. Now you have it, and you don't want it. It goes in the closet.

19

The voice inside has always asked you for one thing only, and that is peace, tranquility, and not another thing after that. Not a third, not a fourth, not a fifth. Only one request. It has been there ever since you were a little child, and it will be there for as long as you are alive, asking you to be content.

This is the story of your life. Maybe it is nothing new. Actually, this is ancient, and, wow, is it exciting! Be excited to know that peace is within you and always will be within you. Be excited to know that this is *your* opportunity. Be excited to know that the greatest of all miracles has taken place. You are alive. Alive.

Change your scales. Do you want to know the definition of *success*? Success is opportunity observed—opportunity taken. Opportunity observed—opportunity not taken: that's failure. Success? Look at yourself. You are the success.

Every breath that comes into you is the great reminder. It's the beat of that drum, of that symphony: You are alive. You exist. It's the kindest, most gentle reminder one could possibly ever have. And in that is your peace.

ON THE WALL OF YOUR HEART
The first priority is that you should have peace in your life. Period. That's it. Look for peace, search for peace, do whatever you have to do for peace.

I'm not selling anything. You need peace in your life. That's what I remind you of because you've got a big agenda now. You're an important person because of the big agenda. That's true. God forbid that big agenda becomes too small. You won't be so important. I'm here to tell you, "You are important regardless of that agenda because you are alive. It is the greatest miracle; it is the greatest gift. And it has been given to you." Given.

Don't say, "Who gave it to me?" Take it. It's given. If you want to be successful in your life, you have to be an opportunist. If you see this life as an opportunity for peace, then take it. If you see this existence as an opportunity to be content, then take it. That is success. The plaque on the wall of your office—that's not success. The plaque on the wall of your heart—that is success.

On the wall of your heart, frame this beautiful poetry that awakens you every day and inspires you to take in more of that opportunity of the beautiful peace that is possible in your life. That's what's important.

If you want peace, peace is possible. But begin turning the radio down, this radio that goes, "Yap, yap, yap." Turn that radio down and listen to the sweet voice that has always been there in your life—a voice calling out for you to be content. And be content.

20

CAPTURE THE DAY

For some people, it's very important to capture what they call "this moment that will only come once." It might be their child's first birthday or graduation day, or this day or that day. Their understanding is that it only happens once, so they'll bring their camera to capture their child's first word or first birthday.

Once, I was watching a reality TV show where people stand in front of a judge and present their grievances. A woman was getting married, and she went to a lot of trouble to make sure that everything was perfect. Of course, you can surmise from the fact that she was on the show that things didn't go very well. A bit of a problem happened, and she was really, really angry: "It took so long to get everything just right, and then this guy came along, and he did this, and he did that." And the poor man says, "Well, I'm sorry, but . . ."

We find these things amusing. We see a mother or father freaking out and saying, "Get that picture, get that picture. My flash didn't go off. Get new batteries . . ." People go through all this because it's so important to capture that moment.

But did you know that this life is also a one-time event? What provisions do you have to capture it? This is something to think about. We buy a camera to capture one of the events in a lifetime. But what do we have to capture a lifetime itself, which is also only going to happen once?

The truth of the matter is, we have no resources for that. We don't look at it that way. We refuse to believe that life is a one-time event.

Let me be a little more precise about this one-time event. Zoom in. This isn't just a question of a lifetime being a one-time event. Every breath is a one-time event. The breath you just took is never, ever coming back again.

I'm not trying to scare you. It's not scary; it's profound. When the world scares you, it's not profound. The difference is that one scares you and the other makes you realize something.

I'm not trying to scare you. I'm just pointing out the obvious—that the breath you just took is not coming back. And you can do something about it. There are tools to go inside and savor the moment, and when you have, you've captured it. When, at the end of the day, your heart is full of gratitude, you just captured the day. You didn't waste it. When your life was lived in gratitude, you didn't waste it. You captured it. That's how simple and profound it is when I allow the moment to touch my heart, when I allow my consciousness to be there. When I accept. Not reject—but accept!

WHERE ARE YOU?
You wake up in the morning to a new day. Good things will happen, and bad things will happen. A day is very much like that. Not everything will be how you want it. Even if it's your birthday, it's not going to be exactly how you want it to be.

Let's say an hour represents a day. A few good things, a few bad things; dull moments, bright moments; action, no action; surge of action, flood of action; frustration, calmness. Then let's say a day represents a week, a week a month, a month a year, and a year a lifetime.

Things will happen, but it is not what happens that is important. What is important is where you are at. There can be chaos, and if you've had a good sleep, your stomach is full, and everything happens to be pretty much okay with you, it's all right. No big deal. Even getting a ticket or missing your flight would be okay: "Ha, ha, ha—I missed my flight."

It's how *you* are that matters. That's just the way it is. If you haven't had a good night's sleep, or if you're hungry or you're running late, then you don't need a ticket or a missed flight to feel terrible. Anything will do it. It could be that you went to the bathroom and there was no more toilet paper. Now, when you really think about it, could a bit of tissue have a devastating impact on your life? If you missed your coffee, do you think your whole world would fall apart? Logically, no. Illogically, yes.

How does that happen? It's simple. When the gears are grinding inside of me, what difference does it make if everything else is running smoothly?

Things will happen, but it is not what happens that is important.

What is important is where you are at.

If your car gets a flat tire, do you look around to see if anybody else has one? If your car runs out of gas, do you look around and ask, "Has anybody else run out of gas?" No. You know it relates only to you. Your running out of gas doesn't mean that everybody on the same road is also going to run out of gas. That sounds stupid, doesn't it? But that's what people do in their lives.

Something happens because their internal gears are grinding, and they look around to see if anybody else's gears are grinding: "Let all the people whose gears are grinding come together and share the experience" so they can feel relieved that they are not the only idiot on the planet. Here, camaraderie counts.

When the gears are grinding inside, what difference do you think camaraderie would make? Peace is not an object that grows on a tree or something that is going to appear in a box on an altar in your house. Peace is something that has to happen for *you*. For the world to be okay, you have to fix the gear inside of you that's grinding. You don't have to fix the world.

Some people think you have to fix the world. "It's the world's fault. So, fix the world, and I'll be okay." No. Do you really think it would help if you took ten gallons of gas and put it in everybody else's car except yours? Of course not. Put that ten gallons in *your* car. That's all you have to do.

This is serious because life is a one-time event. It's not going to come again. And the point of life is not that it only comes once. The point is to be fulfilled.

THIS HEART IS MY FRIEND
It's not about a threat but about recognizing the reality of the situation and doing something about it rather than getting distracted. So much that you do is merely a distraction. Maybe you don't think of it that way, but maybe that's how it is.

The priority of the heart is quite clear. I thank God for the heart, because without it, what would my life be? Where would my sanity be? What could I truly understand? How would I know when I am satisfied? How would I know when I am content?

I would be like a goldfish. Those things can eat until they explode. Right outside my office, I have quite a large pond. The fish in it know when somebody's coming, and they just look up at them, moving their mouths out of the water as if to say, "Feed me, feed me." It doesn't even matter if you feed them. If you turn around and walk back, they'll do the same thing: "Feed me." There's food everywhere, but they look at you like, "Feed me."

Without this heart, where would I be? This heart is my intelligence. This heart is my sanity.

24

Did you know that life is a one-time event? Zoom in. Every breath is a one-time event.

I have two friends. One is my heart, and the other is my mind. One friend says to me, "You have the right to be conscious. You have the right to be kind. You have the right to be fulfilled." And my other friend says, "You have the right to be unconscious. You have the right to be angry. You have the right to be mean."

Two friends in this world. One would be called *bad company*. And the other one? *Good company*.

THE GREATEST TRUTH
Take it one step further. Keep the companionship of truth. People have made truth out to be horrible. Somebody comes to us in tears, and we say, "Tell me the truth. What happened?" Parents do that to their kids. They know the kid stole whatever is missing. They just want the kid to say it.

Is that "truth"? No, truth—the real truth—lies within you. Unwavering. Unchangeable. Undefinable. You cannot speak it, but you can experience it within you. Beautiful. Amazing. Uplifting. And the greatest truth for you as a human being can be none other than to be fulfilled. Then every breath is filled with gratitude, and no matter what you do, you know where you are connected.

When you are connected to that truth within, you become like a mother with a newborn baby. Wherever she goes, her attention is with the baby. Whether she is watching TV or she goes into the kitchen, her attention is with the baby. It doesn't matter what is happening; if she hears the faintest cry from the baby, she will drop everything and go there.

You have the right to be conscious.
You have the right to be kind.
You have the right to be fulfilled.

That's how *you* need to be, too. Whether you are driving a car, flying an airplane, or diving underwater, be connected to that inner place. That is the most ideal position you can put yourself in.

THE PRIZE IS FULFILLMENT

The consequences are nice because there is joy and gratitude, and the day is not wasted. You have allowed your heart to fill with gratitude. You have allowed your heart to fill with that feeling. You have captured the day. You've allowed the breath to be captured. The heart is your camera. Capture the moment. It won't come back again. Be. Exist. Flourish. Enjoy. Simplicity awaits you.

The prize is peace. That is the greatest prize that can ever be—to have fulfilled a human life. Can you think of any greater blessing? That is to be blessed. One breath comes, and it's a blessing. You just got touched.

Do you realize that the moment the breath fills you with life is the shortest distance there will ever be between the finite and infinite? It is the shortest possible line that can be drawn between the two extremes. Into this finite being, the infinite came. You got touched. In that moment, you are a part of the universe. You're not separated from it. You are living; you exist. That's what this whole universe is about.

You want a miracle? The fact that you exist is a miracle. You existed yesterday. That's a miracle. You got up this morning. What a miracle! When you sit there listening to me talk about it, it makes sense. Then you leave here thinking, "Me? Miracle? No way. I want a miracle. God, here is my lottery ticket. Make it win, and that'll be a real miracle."

If you do not know the value of what you have, then "empty-handed you came into the world, and empty-handed you will go" becomes your truth. That's a shame. Even though you came empty-handed, you certainly don't have to go empty-handed.

That feeling is being given, not only once, but in abundance. You can never run out of it. You can definitely have enough anger to kill you, but you will never die of kindness. The feeling within is given to you with no limits. Take as much as you want from that treasure. It is the one thing that most people have the least of in their lives. Talk about irony.

Fulfillment is not limited by your age, your gender, your height, your weight, how much education you have—not by anything. Fulfillment is fulfillment, and it is being given freely to every human being on Earth.

28

DUALITY STOPS, SINGULARITY BEGINS

Bring acceptance into your life. What is acceptance? To receive the gift that is being given without standing over it and saying, "Let me alter this." You don't alter a sunset. You don't alter a crescent moon or a full moon.

When you accept each breath, it becomes different, subtle, simple, joyous—and the heart is the judge. It is silent without the absence of sound. It *is*. And it is within you. It is a breath, and it's so much more. It is where duality stops and singularity begins. It is the only place where there is a distinct separation between feeling and thought, where the mind cannot actually think about what you are feeling because it is beyond its perception.

A great duality is created. And in that duality, you pick a side. When you pick the side of the heart, when you pick the side of that feeling inside, you will notice the singularity.

This is where answers begin to come, but there are no questions. It's unique. You have the answers, but you don't have the questions. This is where you are fulfilled, but you were never hungry. This is where your thirst has been quenched, but you were never thirsty. This is where you are, without being. You become one. The doubts are no longer there if there is acceptance, if there is understanding.

This is the pulse of life. Go inside and experience that, because there is nothing like it. Nothing.

When, at the end of the day, your heart is full of gratitude, you just captured the day.

You have a potential to discover yourself.
Dig the mine within you. Quench the thirst.
Fulfill the potential. Come home.

THE
POTENTIAL

What I talk about boils down to this: What is the possibility for a human being in life? And what I want to tell you about does not reside on top of a mountain or at the bottom of the ocean; it is something that resides in the heart of each and every person in this world.

So, what is the potential of a human life—of my life, of your life?

You hold a seed in your hand. In that seed is a tree. And in that tree are many, many more seeds. And in each one of those seeds is another tree. In those trees, there are thousands more seeds and thousands more trees, and soon, you're looking at millions and millions of trees. Just looking at a single seed sitting in the palm of your hand, you're looking at the beginning of a very large forest.

The seed has that possibility. If that seed is sown, watered, taken care of, it could become a tree, and from that tree could come a forest. But if the seed is *not* planted and taken care of, where is the possibility of the forest? It does not exist and will not exist.

DORMANT POSSIBILITY
What I'm trying to say is this: Peace lies dormant in the heart of every single person, but something has to change before that potential will be realized. Unless that happens, it remains just a possibility. You can write poems or books about it, you can have seminars about it, but it's only a possibility; it's not a reality.

I've been talking about peace in so many different places. I've been saying we need peace even in the absence of war. War starts, and everybody says, "We should have peace; we should have peace." And what happens when the war stops? "Oh yes, let's go back to business as usual." What kind of business? The business that takes us to war! Peace is not something you can merely talk about. It is not as though you can just put a placard on a wall or hold up two fingers and then have peace.

Peace is something that has to be *felt*—not once, not twice, not three times, but every day, every moment that it's possible to feel it. That is why I am talking to you. I'm not just telling you about the possibility. I'm also pointing out that it can become a *reality* in your life.

To a thirsty person, what good is a pep talk? Imagine a person is dying of thirst in the desert, and you're saying, "I know a great place in London that has incredible water." You're telling him about a water bar, which offers all different kinds of water. He's just saying, "Water, water."

You can talk about peace all you want when the *need* is not present. But when the need is present, there is no room for discussion. You want one thing and only one thing: to fulfill the need. This is how you are made.

Peace lies dormant
in the heart of every single person...

32

IS PEACE A NECESSITY?

You have the capacity to contemplate, to think, to imagine. You can do an incredible job with these abilities. But that does not replace taking care of your necessities. Your thirst needs to be quenched.

Only when your thirst is quenched does the chapter of thirst come to a conclusion, and not a moment sooner. None of the discoveries, the reading, or all the ideas in the world can make a difference if the thirst is not quenched. This is how it is. The ability to imagine does not take away necessity. You will not be satisfied until you have consumed the water and your thirst has been taken away.

So, then, the obvious question is, do you have a need in your life to be fulfilled? That's a question you have to ask yourself and answer for yourself. In my life? Yes. I have a need to feel peace, to be fulfilled, to be satisfied in the most fundamental way. And not the satisfaction that comes from somebody saying, "This is your new mantra: 'I'm satisfied; I'm satisfied; I'm satisfied.'" Some people do that. They say, "Start to tell yourself how happy you are, and you will become happy." There's one problem with that happiness—it's imagined.

If that's what you're doing, God forbid you actually start feeling the *need* to be happy. You have told yourself, "Be happy, be happy, be happy." Then one day, something inside of you says, "That's a good idea; I really should be happy." And then you find yourself in *big* trouble, because you thought you were already taking care of it.

People say, "What about all the responsibilities that we have?" I don't see a conflict, because the happiness you are looking for is the happiness that lies within you, for *you*—just as a person who is alive, who came into being. I know that it might be difficult to disassociate yourself from being a father or a mother, a teacher or a farmer, a this or a that. But do, just for a second.

BREATH COMES INTO ME

You came into existence. Breath came into you, and it's yours. It doesn't matter how charitable you are; you cannot give it away. I can't say, "Here's a few of my breaths. It's a gift to you." I can't do that. Breath comes into *me*, brings me something, and leaves. And it comes again and leaves, comes again and leaves, till one day it comes, leaves, and doesn't come back again.

…but something has to change before the potential will be realized.

There is a home within you ...

People don't like to talk about that; it gets heavy, intense. Take a look at your birthday. Your family or friends bring a cake. They put candles on the cake and then say, "Here. Blow them out." Each one of those candles represents a year that you've been alive. So you are symbolically blowing away each one of those years.

You are accepting the passage of all of those years—it's done. Of course, nobody knows how long you're going to live, so they couldn't put on the additional candles. The blowing out of candles is about your vulnerability, not your strength. The illusion is the song that goes along with it. That's truly distracting. It makes you think blowing out the candles is about your future, but really it is the acceptance of all that's gone and will never come back. And that is the nature of your life.

Don't judge whether that is good or bad, right or wrong, or whether it should be some other way. It is the nature of existence. It's simple. You are here, and being alive is your *greatest* celebration. You don't look at it that way, because you have scales. Everything is weighed and measured, and it's either a good time or a bad time. You measure yourself—not by *your* state but by the state of things around you. Is your business doing well? Are you getting a promotion? Have you been passed up for a promotion? That would make a bad day. Your business not doing so well would also make a bad day. And what makes a good day? When things are going your way—because you measured the day by that. You didn't accept the day; you measured it.

ART OF MERGING
I'm talking about accepting life and accepting the need to be fulfilled. To be in joy. Not because somebody told you, "Now you are successful; now you are happy; now you are in joy," but feeling a joy that comes from the very depths of your own being. Being happy because you are fulfilled and you accept today as a gift, because it *is* a gift.

What is a gift? When somebody gives you something and asks nothing in return, it becomes a gift. When somebody gives you something and says, "Where's your credit card?" it is no longer a gift. When I say, "Life is a gift," immediately some people think, "Who is it from?" Do you really care? It's being given. Take it. Are you going to fight it?

What did you give for today? Nothing. But it came, and all the moments were like little drops. A drop of water merges with another drop of water. That's another example of potential. If another drop comes by, the water droplet has the possibility to merge with it, and if another one comes, it will merge with that one, too. Another

... and you need to come home.

one comes by, and it will merge with that one, too. This possibility of merging allows it to become a mighty river. If each drop said, "I don't know where this other drop came from; I don't know what its convictions are, what its religion is, what it believes in, so I'm not going to join it," the river would never be.

Water knows how to transform itself. Heat it, and it says, "Oh, this is too hot. I'm leaving," and it evaporates. Does it go away? No. Any moment it can collect itself, it will. It will become a drop again, coming right back as water to join the ocean. Sometimes it can rain and rain. And what is rain? It is the droplet making use of its potential. The droplet is tiny, but it can cut a mountain in half. I'm fascinated by this.

Water is so supple, and yet, those drops coming together have the potential to generate megawatts of electricity. From a very simple thing that it wants to do, which is to flow toward a lower area, mega-megawatts of electricity are generated. All because a drop knows the art of merging with another drop. That is its nature.

THE WAR INSIDE

When can I begin to understand that *my* nature is to feel? To think is okay, but I need to feel. To imagine is okay, but I need to see. To have a dream is all right, but I need to be fulfilled with my eyes open. There is nothing wrong with dreaming, but fulfillment has to be the biggest part of it. When I can understand that today is a gift that was given to me without judgment, when I can accept it, then I will have taken the very first step on the ladder to fulfilling myself. Then I will know that I am going in the direction of being in peace.

When you talk to most people about peace, they say, "When there is no war, that's peace." No. That's not peace. War is a consequence of something. There isn't just the physical war. There is another war that is far more dangerous, and that is the war that rages on inside a human being. The war on the outside will end sooner or later. But the war inside can rage on and on with no end in sight.

In the world today, we have departments of war, departments of defense. How about a department of peace? Not to be found. Peace is seen as just a good idea, not something we should actually have. Billions of dollars are spent on weapons. When it comes time to collect taxes, governments boast about the accuracy of these weapons. But when they blow up half of the wrong place, you wonder, "I thought this was supposed to be hyperaccurate stuff that could come through one window and leave through another window. What happened?" It found the wrong window!

IN TOUCH WITH YOURSELF

If I ask somebody, "When was the last time you were truly in touch with yourself?" they might answer, "I'm not perfect, but you know, I try. I'm a good person. I don't mean to harm anyone." No. Not like that, not in thought. In feeling.

Who are you? You are a unique being who came into this life. There's no one like you in the whole world, and there will never be anyone like you, ever. That's how unique you are. That's why it is important to be fulfilled.

We think, "I'm sure there's somebody like me." We even go around saying, "I saw somebody who looked just like you." It's not true. The way you see, the way you laugh, what you laugh at, and what makes you smile are the incredibly subtle nuances of your existence. When you are fulfilled, the way you feel is the subtle texture of life. Incredibly subtle. So subtle that only you would be able to tell what it is all about. Therefore, it is incumbent upon you to be fulfilled. It is so important that this materialization of flesh and blood that came onto this earth did not go to waste. That you didn't just come here and leave one day. But you came here, you saw, you admired, you were fulfilled.

Will you be remembered ten years after you leave? Well, maybe ten. Maybe twenty. Thirty? I don't know. It is the nature of the world to forget. Even if they erected a statue of you, one day somebody will come along and want to build an apartment building there, and off you will go. That's not what your life is about. That's not your potential.

Ultimately, what you are dependent upon is not all the things you think you are dependent upon. What you are dependent upon, in fact, is the breath that comes in and goes out. If it ever came down to trading your cell phone, your computer, or your new watch for your breath, you would gladly say, "Here. Take it, take it!" because you know that breath is your pillar, your foundation.

KNOWING YOURSELF

You should know the benefit of quenching your thirst, of being in peace. No one is that far removed. But we do need a reminder. When we can forget what is absolutely essential, we can do with a reminder. What I talk about is knowing yourself. Businesses will come and go, but you are one and only one. This life is about being fulfilled, being in joy, digging the mine within you, quenching the thirst. It is about coming home. There is a home within you, and you need to come home.

There is a potential for you to discover and to know yourself. Fulfill your potential.

FACT NUMBER ONE

Because you exist, you will make a voyage. What will this voyage be like? You don't know. No one knows. You are given a vessel—the human body—and by the very fact that it breathes, that it exists, it will make a voyage. It will go where truly no one has gone before.

You might say, "Isn't my voyage going to be very similar to the person sitting next to me?" No. Because there are infinite little variables, and that will make your voyage unlike anyone else's. How you perceive, how you think, how you understand, is completely unique to you.

STATISTICS AND REALITY

We tend to generalize, and everything becomes an average, but if you go a little bit beyond the average, you will realize that all the numbers are unique.

When driving somewhere, your risk of having a flat tire is maybe only 0.01 percent. Fine. But what if you *do* have one? It wouldn't help you to say, "I didn't bring a spare tire because there was a 99.99 percent chance that I would *not* get a flat."

When you average, you preclude reality. And reality is what you have to deal with every single day, not averages. What will your day be like today? What will your day be like tomorrow? Even if you have the same job and you do the same things every day, no two days will be alike. So what do these averages represent? Nothing. Only after you die can those numbers be calculated to say, "Right. These numbers actually agree with this person's averages, because he or she had two years' worth of a really bad time, five years' worth of a really good time," and so on.

But while you are alive, every day is different. It is not just a question of good or bad—it is a question of how you view the good and bad. One day things could actually be really terrible, but you view them as good because you're feeling good inside, so you say, "It's okay; it's not so bad."

Then there could be another day where things are actually going really well, but you're not feeling good inside, so you think, "Oh, no. What's the point? Everything is bad." It is all variable.

POINT ZERO

So, how do you make this voyage? Who are you? What is the purpose of the voyage? And why does it have to be made?

To understand this, you have to begin at point zero. Not point one hundred. You've heard a lot. You have read a lot of books. You have a lot of information floating in your head—like who God is and where God is. Don't you? "Where is God?" Everyone points and says, "Up there." Then you're told that if you do good things, you will go to heaven; if you do bad things, you will end up in hell. Hell is terrible. You don't want to go there. Heaven is good. You do want to go there. And so you should be like this and like that, and if you do all these good things, you *will* get to heaven.

All this information is floating around in your head. That's why you need to begin at point zero—with no information. And then look at facts, not ideas. Fact number one: you are alive. And who are you?

You always try to make yourself comfortable. You want a soft bed. You want a nice, soft pillow. Maybe you don't want to go searching for water at night when you get

38

Begin at point zero with no information. And then look at facts, not ideas.

Fact number one: you are alive!

Who are you?

thirsty, so you put a bottle of water next to your bed. You don't want to sit there and wonder what time it is, so you put a little clock by your bed.

What do you do when you go to buy shoes? You don't just walk into the store and say, "Give me a pair of shoes." You try them on. And then you walk a little bit. Why? To make sure that the shoes have not been worn before? No. You walk in those shoes to make sure they're comfortable. When you go to buy glasses, you don't say, "Just give me a pair of glasses." No. First you try them on to see how they fit. And then you look in the mirror to see how they look.

When it gets hot, you are uncomfortable, so what do you do? If you can't avoid the heat, you might use a book or a booklet as a fan. Anything will do because you have to get comfortable.

We spend a lot of time and energy making sure our body is comfortable. The question is, do we also spend time to make sure that our *existence* is comfortable? Or do we learn how to live with disparity, how to live with anger, how to live with confusion?

If this is what we are doing, it would be akin to buying a pair of shoes that has a nail sticking into the foot. When you put them on, they hurt, but they look good, so you say, "Perfect. This is what I want." It cannot be like that.

We don't like pain. We will do whatever is necessary to get rid of pain. This is our nature. You talk, think, see, hear, taste, smell. And you also like to smell that which brings you enjoyment. Bad smell? Instantly you say, "Ugh." Good smell, you say, "Mmmm."

What do you like to hear? That which brings you enjoyment. What do you like to see? That which brings you enjoyment. This is how you are. This is who you are—make no mistake about it.

THE ULTIMATE EXPERIENCE
Just looking at these facts, it seems to me that we are here to enjoy. You want to enjoy everything you do—and you *should* enjoy everything you do. What does your heart want to do? It also wants to enjoy. And what can your heart enjoy? This is the question.

We have been given a body that loves to enjoy. It doesn't matter who we are or what circumstances we are in, we always want to be comfortable. And we also want to be comfortable inside of us. So perhaps the purpose of this voyage of life is not pain and suffering, but to be able to experience the ultimate experience. Now.

What do you think the ultimate experience is? I would have to say that the experience of the ultimate is an ultimate experience.

What is the ultimate? The ultimate is the power that makes everything possible —that moves the whole universe.

I'm not going to try to define the ultimate, because one of the definitions of the ultimate is that it's *indefinable*. I'm not going to try to explain what infinity is. You and I cannot understand what infinity is.

And forget about understanding the universe—it is ever-changing. We will never grasp the scale of it. No measurement is big enough.

What is really fascinating is not understanding the universe, but understanding that which powers the universe. It also happens to be within us—and we can experience it. Why should you experience it? This is where it gets really beautiful. Because when you experience the ultimate, you get filled with peace. When you do, you get filled with clarity. When you do, you get filled with joy. When you do, you experience the truest, truest happiness.

40

We spend a lot of time and energy to make sure our body is comfortable.

Do we also spend time to make sure our existence is comfortable?

Those sound like very good reasons. So, when I look at this voyage of life and understand what it can make possible, I really want to take the voyage.

PRESENCE AND ABSENCE

What do you need on the voyage? Do you need anger? Do you need fear? They have been given to you, but so has kindness. There's confusion, but there's also clarity. There is pain, but there is also joy. And it's very important to know which one is an absence and which one is a presence.

Darkness is not a presence. It is just the absence of light. Cruelty is not a presence. It's just the absence of kindness. Pain is not a presence. It's just the absence of joy. Suffering is not a presence. It's just the absence of peace.

In many civilizations, people prayed to the sun. The sun was very important to them. It brought warmth, light, life, so they prayed to it. But they couldn't do very much in the dark. Well, light removes darkness!

We learn that Edison invented the lightbulb, but the understanding that light removes darkness existed way before him. That's why people used to light fires at night. You don't have to make a machine that removes darkness, because darkness in itself is nothing. Bring light, and darkness will go away. Bring joy, and pain will go away. Bring clarity, and doubts will go away. Is it that easy? Yes.

YOUR "NOT" LIST

To remove the doubts is impossible, but to bring clarity into your life is very possible. Do you have a list of the things that you do *not* want in your life or the things that you *do* want? It's a very good question, because most people do not even have one single item of what they *do* want on their list. It's all what they don't want: "I don't want confusion. I don't want poverty. I don't want pain. I don't want this. I don't want that."

Maybe you say, "God, I don't want to get lost." "God, I don't want to go to hell." "God, save me from pain and suffering." Wrong prayers. You are trying to invent the darkness-removing machine. Your prayer should be, "I want to experience heaven now." Not, "Don't send me to hell." What is hell? It is all that heaven isn't. Hell is not a presence. It's just the absence of heaven!

If I want to build a house, and I say to the architect, "Let me show you all the houses I don't want my house to look like," how many photographs would that take? How many tours would have to be made? I would be saying, "Let's go and explore the southeast section of the city, where I will show you all the houses that I don't want my house to look like. Not that, not that, not that..."

The poor architect would say, "What can I do with a list of nots? I need a list of what you *do* want." So what do you *want* in your life? You want peace. Why? Because it feels so good. You want joy because it feels so good. You want clarity; you want understanding. And you want to feel your heaven. *Now*!

LIGHTEN YOUR LOAD

Many people say, "I am not enjoying my voyage. It's terrible." Of course. You have overpacked. You can't carry your luggage; it's too heavy. Your back hurts from carrying all those ideas. Lighten your load. Carry the essentials; they are all that you will need. Clarity will see you through most problems. That's how clarity is.

It's really amazing. Confusion, even though it's an absence, weighs so much that its weight is almost incalculable. Clarity weighs so little that when it comes to you, you hardly feel any weight. Have you noticed that?

Pain weighs so much. And joy? It weighs so little that it even makes you feel lighter. These are good things to carry with you, because they hardly weigh anything, and they make you lighter, too. You get the best of both worlds.

This is the possibility. Take the voyage. Don't be shy. It's a good voyage. Feel heaven here, now. It's no mystery. Your existence on this earth was designed for you to be in peace, to be in joy.

WHAT IS THIS "I"?

Most of what we hear in our lives is either about how things were or how they could be. Especially when we get older, we think about how it used to be when we were young. On many occasions, I have heard people actually say, "Oh, when I was young, I used to do this and I used to do that, and when we were young, we used to go here and we used to go there."

So much memory, so much thought is dedicated to what was. Where do we derive our hopes and aspirations from? They come from what might be. That's what we work for. We look to the future, and in the future, we try to see what would be good and how it could come to be. We take our dreams, our aspirations, our ideas, and we say, "I will work hard. I will do this. I will acquire that. And then one day, someday in the future, I'll be happy. I'll be content."

I talk about another dimension, another time. This time is not in the past, and it is not in the future. The time I talk about is *now*. In this moment, in this very second, the breath that comes into you is heralding the possibility of immeasurable joy. This is what is so interesting: in this moment called *now*, all my wants and my wishes are being fulfilled.

The question that arises is, who is this person saying "my," saying "me"? Who is this "I"? To answer that, we have to begin to understand what our existence is all about.

THE FUNDAMENTAL UNDERSTANDING

Let's think of a man. His job is to make frames. People bring him their paintings—beautiful paintings—and he makes frames. This is all he does. He makes frames, and he frames pictures. And he's very good. As his popularity spreads, more people bring him their pictures, and he is busy day and night, framing, framing, framing. All these paintings that come to him are magnificent, but, alas, he has no time to look at them and admire them because he is too busy framing. When a picture comes, he doesn't look at it. He measures the width, and he measures the height; he cuts the frame, and with his hammer and nails, he frames the picture. And he says, "Next" and "Next" and "Next." When, after hours of framing, he is tired, he says, "Now I must rest."

He leaves his workshop, goes outside, looks all around, and says, "Oh, I'm so tired." So he takes his tea or coffee break. Then he looks at his watch and goes back. And what does he do? "Next." Measures it, frames it. "Next." Measures it, frames it. And that's what happens.

That's what all of us do. Because the concern is—and this is a statement made by so many people—"What will I do with my time?" Let's look at that. Forget about "what" for a minute, forget about "will," and forget about "do." "I" and "my time"—that's what's important. That is what it is all about.

I hear people saying, "I love the color blue." Somebody else says, "I love orange," or "I love green." The main thing in these statements is not the color. It is the "I," because without the "I," you can have all the colors you want, but nobody to say, "I love." It is this "I" that allows you to be a father, a mother, a wife, a teacher, a pilot, a doctor, a lawyer, or whoever you are. Whatever you are, it is this "I" that allowed you to have a job, to be a child, to play; it is this "I" that allowed you—and will allow

44

you—to retire. One day the "I" will be no more, and then . . . I don't have to say it. You know. When the "I" is finished, none of it matters any longer.

What does matter, though, is whether you recognized the "I" in the "I." Did you recognize the "I" that allows you to be everything you are and will allow you to be everything you will be? What is that "I"?

THE FORMULA

What is the breath? What is this life? What is this existence? When I have it, I have everything, and when I don't have it, I have nothing—and not even nothing. I don't have to work for it. I don't have to earn it. I have it. What do I have?

It begins with the understanding of this "I"—this *you*! And the fundamental understanding of you is all about understanding what you *have*. The world always tells you what you could have. Every advertisement is about what you *could* have. Not what you *need*. What you *could* have.

When I have it, I have everything.

When I don't have it, I have nothing.

The world tells you what you must do to be happy, but it never shows you a person who did all of that and was happy. The formula the world gives you has no equal sign at the end. It's just a formula. What does it equal? What does it produce? What does it do? Nobody knows. "Do all of this, do all of that. . . ." I'm not criticizing anything. I am saying the key ingredient missing in all that is happening in the world is *you*. I am saying it because, in your life, you have all your responsibilities, but you also have the responsibility of recognizing what you have been given.

You have ears. And I am sure that so many of you have listened to beautiful concerts and enjoyed them very much. Beautiful symphonies. Beautiful violins, harps, pianos. And you said, "Wow! This is beautiful." I'm sure you have heard a lot of lectures, and you have thought about them and discussed them over a cup of coffee, asking, "What did you think of this? What did you think of that?"

45

Now, let me ask you another question: Have you heard the call of your heart? No poetry was ever written as sweet as the call of the heart. If there was ever a perfect lecture, it is the lecture of the heart. And if there is a voice that is sweet, then it is the voice of the heart. Listen to it. Pay attention because something so sweet is manifesting in your life. Listen to the request because it is about peace, it is about joy, it is about being fulfilled. Not tomorrow. Not the day after tomorrow. Now. To be complete now.

ALMOST COMPLETE
Yesterday I was speaking at a university, and one of the things I was talking about was "almost complete." Not complete, *almost* complete.

When I come and speak, I don't have a prewritten speech. So when I said what I said yesterday, it was as much of a surprise to me as it was to the audience. And afterward I was thinking about "almost complete." The painting that is *almost* complete does not express what it could. Its potential has not been realized. The song that is *almost* complete does not express what the writer wants to express.

In our lives, we, too, are almost complete. It's like the bridge that is magnificent but has another eight feet to go. Nobody can use it because it's not complete. It's almost complete. It's like a jacket or dress that is missing the sleeves. You can't wear it. Or the pasta that is *almost* complete, you can't eat it.

I talk about another dimension, another time. This time is not in the past, and it is not in the future. This time is now.

How do *you* become complete? What does it take to complete this existence? It's so simple. Recognize what you have been given. Recognize! That's all you have to do. After that, what will happen is automatic. The farmer can only sow the seed. He cannot squeeze the seed and make it sprout. If he starts doing that, he will kill everything. All he can do is sow it. All I can do is recognize. And then the unfolding begins. This is what knowledge of the self is all about.

KNOWLEDGE OF YOURSELF

People ask, "What is so important about self-knowledge?" Here is a good analogy: You live in Madrid, and you know a lot of addresses—you know the café, the movie theater, the office building, the supermarket, and the airport. Of all those addresses, which one is the most important? Where you live is the most important address. You may go to the supermarket one day and not go another day, but you want to be home every day.

It doesn't matter where you go in the world; you want to come back home. You really do. Think about it. Let's say you have worked really hard, and you have bought a ticket for your holiday. What are you doing at home? You're doing all the preparation so you can go and have your vacation. But—most importantly—you want to come back home. If somebody said, "You can go, but you can't come back," you would say, "I'm not leaving. I'm staying home."

Home is *me*. I may acquire a lot of knowledge, and much of it I may never need.

How do you become complete?
It's so simple.
Recognize what you have been given.

Things will change. But as long as I am me, I will need to have knowledge of my own self. *Me.* As long as breath comes into this body and this instrument plays the sweet song of life, I want to be there to listen. I want to be there to dance to that rhythm, that tune, that joy, that breath, that understanding.

A lot of people have a mantra: "Smile, smile, smile." People are told, "Look good. Smile." And they have to remember, "Smile, smile, smile." It is hard if there is nothing to smile about. Sooner or later, you will forget the mantra, and as soon as you forget the mantra, you go back to frowning. The smile is gone. So people write it everywhere, "Smile, smile, smile." But sooner or later, your eyesight will be gone. "What's written on the wall? I don't know. I forgot." See what I am saying?

There is something that is variable by nature, and it will stay variable. So much is changing around me all the time. My eyesight? Not as good as it used to be. My hearing? Not as good as it used to be. Smell? I think it's still very good, but it is changing, and it will change and change. But do you know what has not changed?

The breath coming into me and the call of my heart have always been the same. Not a single beat has been missed. The call of the heart has always been, "Be fulfilled. In every *moment*, be fulfilled."

People say to me, "That's very hard." The question isn't whether it is easy or hard. Just know that in every breath lies the possibility of being fulfilled. Whether you accept it or not is not the point. The point is that the possibility is there.

A lot of people have come here today to listen to what I have to say, and I thank you very much for coming because you also have the possibility of having your life fulfilled.

Now, a lot of you are going to walk away from here and say, "I did not understand a word he said. I feel pretty fulfilled." How do you know you're fulfilled? I will tell you. The day that call of the heart changes from, "Be fulfilled" to "Thank you" is the day you will know you are fulfilled.

SEARCHING

Last night I was thirsty. The room was dark, and I could not see. So I'm looking for the flashlight. I turn on the flashlight. I see the bottle of water, open it, and drink, drink, drink; then I stopped because my thirst was quenched.

Let's change this example: The room is dark. I know there is a flashlight, and I'm looking for it so I can turn it on and see where the bottle of water is. The point is to find the water. I'm only looking for the flashlight so I can see the water. Next thing I know, I turn on the room light. Now I can see the bottle of water, but I'm still looking for the flashlight. Why am I still looking for the flashlight? Because I forgot that the reason I was looking for the flashlight was to see the water. Now an even bigger light has gone on, and I'm still looking for the flashlight. I can't find the flashlight, so I'm not drinking the water, and I am still thirsty. Does that sound familiar?

Why have we created what we have created? To be fulfilled. Is it fulfilling us? No. Are we still chasing it? Yes. And how long are we going to chase it? So, in the simplest of terms, what I am saying is that what you are looking for, what you have been looking for, and what you will be looking for are all within you.

Where does it all begin? First, listen to the call of your heart. Be quiet. Stop talking. You've been talking, talking, talking. Saying what? "I think I have everything, I think I have everything, I think I have everything." God forbid a day should ever come when you say, "I *thought* I had everything." But you must know. *Know.*

Because it is possible in this life to be fulfilled. Walk in certainty. That's what it takes. That's what life requires, that's what life demands. Walk in certainty, not in uncertainty. Your whole life will change.

The world tells you what you must do to be happy, but it never shows you a person who did all of that and was happy.

You will begin to ask not the value of tomorrow, but the value of today. Your life will change. That's what it takes. It's so close. There is not much of a difference between tomorrow and today. There really isn't. Technically speaking, it's only one second difference, but it makes all the difference in the world because tomorrow is speculation; today is certainty. Walk in certainty. Walk with that thirst. Walk toward the well in your life that will quench the thirst. And if you don't know where the well is, then look within you, not outside. Look within you. You have looked outside for too long. I'm not saying you haven't found many things outside, but remember, you haven't found that one thing you were looking for, that one element that started the search of a lifetime. What is that one element? I'm not going to say it. You already know.

The beating of the drum of breath. I want to hear it again and again and again.

You are the one who is searching. Some people say, "I don't think I am searching." Yes, you are. When you are attracted by a sign on the side of the road, you are searching. When you look at a shop and say, "Mmm," you are searching. When that flashy motorcycle goes by and you look, you are searching. Of course you are searching. When the beautiful full moon shines in the sky and you look at it, you are searching. You are searching, and you will be searching until you have found it.

This is how simple it is. To some people, it's very complicated. Some people ask me, "What about my religion?" Follow your religion. This has nothing to do with your religion. This has to do with you, just you in your journey of life.

Will it make you a better person? I don't know. Will it make you more successful in your business? I don't know. Will it make you more popular with women? With men? I don't know. This much, I *do* know: It will make you very popular with your heart. It will make you very attracted to your heart. That's how simple it is.

YOUR BOOK OF LIFE

Is there a book I preach from? No. Because all you need to read is written in the chapters of your heart. In your heart is a book that has been written, that *will* be written. There is a book that is *being* written. And it's *your* book. Is it interesting? Nobody will know except you because only you get to read your book. Nobody else can read it. So, is it interesting? Well, it depends. Did you pay attention when you were writing it?

I get such a kick out of it. Sometimes, I write a note to myself very fast. And then two days later, I read it and say, "What did I write?" I know I wrote that, but I wasn't paying attention. Now I can't read it. It was something important; that's why I wrote it. I say to myself, "Should have paid more attention. Write slowly, write clearly." What have *you* written in the book of *your* life? Are you having a hard time reading it?

Is that why so many people won't talk about this? They say, "It's okay. There's nothing there." No. Every day, take a little time because the book is being written. It is the book of life; every page is being written. Write it clearly because you're going to have to read it. You're going to want to read it. And, hopefully, it'll be joyful to read because it is your words that will be written. This is the possibility I am talking about.

This is all about joy. It's true joy, joy of the heart. Come from that simple place and you, too, can understand. It is the simplest things in life that carry the greatest meaning. It is the things that we forget about, the things that we start to assume, that bring us pain. When was the last time you told those you really love that you love them?

In this world, fathers forget to tell their children they love them; children forget to tell their fathers they love them. Husbands forget to tell their wives they love them; wives forget to tell their husbands they love them. This forgetting has gone so far that we forget to tell all those we love that we love them. We forget.

So, now is the time to start remembering the possibility that I have talked about. After the thirst has become clear, the purpose of the water also becomes very clear. Until then, without the thirst, it's only speculation. Don't live this life in speculation. Don't live this life in uncertainty. Every step, every breath, should be taken in certainty.

Tomorrow is speculation.
Today is certainty.

Walk in certainty
toward the well
that will quench your thirst.

Because of explanations, we lose the focus of what life is all about.

I'm not talking about referring to a book. I'm talking about you asking yourself:

What is it that I want in this existence?

MORE BEAUTIFUL
THAN ANY FANTASY

Life is always unfolding. Nothing is static. It's always changing. Always moving forward. And we have to learn to move forward with it. Otherwise, we will be left behind. When we look at the world, we see so many people who have been left behind trying to catch up every day, trying to do what is right, trying to be simple by becoming incredibly complicated. This is because we don't understand what simplicity really is. We think that if we give up everything, we will become simple. This is not true.

Some people go to great lengths to announce to the world, "I have renounced. I have given up so many things. And I want to show you that I have given up. I want to tell you that I have given up." But in trying to give up, they haven't given up what they *should* give up. So, what is simplicity?

If I leave my job, will I become simple? No. Because to understand simplicity, we have to understand what is making it complicated. And what is making it complicated? There's a beautiful couplet from an Indian poet from the fifteenth century. He said the infinite is not a topic of conversation. All you can do is feel it. Experience it. And then you will understand.

ARE YOU RESTLESS?
Life needs to be felt. Do you feel alive? When I ask this, people immediately think, "Of course, I am alive because of this and this." But these things are not what make you feel alive.

Somebody said that the drums of the breath beat day and night. A fool sleeps through it, and the one who is awakened is restless because of these drums playing day and night. Now, being restless can be negative—you can be restless if you are bored. Or you can be restless if you are excited and can't wait for something. And *that's* the point. Are you bored and therefore restless? Or are you excited and therefore restless? So restless you cannot wait for the next beat of this drum of breath, cannot wait to hear it again, for it to go through you again. Cannot wait to be mesmerized, to be elated. One more step. One more beat. To dance the dance of life. That is what feeling alive is all about.

Feeling. Understanding what is important in your existence every day. That's what simplicity is all about. Not wondering, "What is going to happen to me? When I die, am I going to heaven?"

People say, "We are here to suffer. And if we suffer enough, then when we die, we will go to heaven." There are incredible ways of suffering on planet Earth: One, live in the desert in the summer without air conditioning. Two, make your home in the North Pole in the winter with no heat in your house. You will suffer.

Because of explanations, we lose the focus of what life is all about. I'm not talking about referring to a book. I'm talking about you referring to *yourself*. About you asking yourself—nobody else—"What is it that I want in my existence?"

This is *your* life. You have been given this opportunity to be alive. In you beats the drum of breath. You have consciousness. You have awareness—or at least the possibility of awareness. You have the possibility to remember, and you have the possibility to forget. You have the good; you have the bad. You have the right; you have the wrong.

56

Ugliness and beauty are not very far away from you. How far? The thickness of a hair. That's a pretty fine line.

My analogy is this: You are in a restaurant. The waiter is coming toward you with an incredible dish. It looks beautiful, and your mouth is watering. You cannot wait to eat it. Then it is in front of you, and just as you pick up your knife and fork, you see there is a hair in the food. Now you don't want it anymore. "Take it back!" you say, because you don't know whose hair it is. This could be a hair from a person who hasn't taken a shower for the last six months. The thickness of a hair, that's how close ugliness and beauty can be for you.

KNOW THE VALUE

In this life, all the possibilities are within you. There are no limits. What do you want? The answer must come from your heart, from that one place in you that is sincere. The answer must come from that same place, whatever you call it, that has been calling out to you, asking, "What is it that you want?"

You think your house belongs to you; it doesn't. The house knows that after you're gone, somebody else will live there. What can you call your own in this world? What is really your own? This breath is your own. It just came and went. It comes again, and it goes. And it comes again. That is your miracle; that is the grace in your life.

How many times have you sat in a room and said, "God, if you're real, I want to see you"? And God came as the breath and blessed you. That is the truest blessing of all.

And he came in no uncertain terms. Not as a face and not as an eye; not as a mouth and not as a tooth. We need eyes so we can see. That power does not need eyes to see. We need a nose to breathe. That power does not need a nose, but we give it a face.

What are you looking for? What do you want? What do you need? You know you have needs, but do you know how many of your needs have already been fulfilled?

Without knowing the value of life, you live in a world of total uncertainty. In ignorance, a human being struggles because he is living in uncertainty. He is not certain about tomorrow. And when a human being is not certain about something, one of two things happens. Either the human being accepts that and says, "I am going to do something about it," or, like most people, the human being makes up a story about tomorrow. Once the story has been made up, a human being will do anything to believe in that story, whatever it takes. But it's a story, and a story does not remove uncertainty.

Knowledge. Knowing. Understanding. These are the only things that can remove uncertainty so that I can begin to welcome what tomorrow is. Not what tomorrow brings, but what tomorrow is. It is the beating of the drum of breath, and I want

Without knowing the value of life, you live in a world of total uncertainty.

to be restless to feel it again, to hear it again, and again and again in my life.

I have a long list of all the things I want on the outside, but my success and failure cannot be dependent upon those things. My success is my restlessness to listen to the drum of my breath.

My yearning. My truest want to feel alive. To feel this existence. To feel the blessing of my God come and touch me. I've been given that blessing. And I want to be blessed again and again and again. I want to be dazzled by that miracle. I want to witness that miracle. In no uncertain terms, existence is an incredible miracle.

People like to make up stories and believe in those stories so, somehow, they can forget about what is happening now. Anything to forget what is happening now. We say, "I'm young, I'm old, I'm poor, I'm rich." Another Indian poet says a simple, beautiful thing: Inside each one of us is the same, just as the light of a lamp will be the same whether the lamp is lit in the house of a beggar, the house of a king, or the house of a saint. It gives the same light.

KNOW YOUR NATURE
We know about our differences. We do not know about our similarity. Every human being wants to feel peace. Every human being wants to feel joy. It doesn't matter what they call it. Don't get caught in semantics. Every human being wants to feel love. Why? Because this is our nature. When we get tired of standing, we like to sit down. And if we can't find a chair, a bench will be fine. A rock, fine. Grass, fine. Asphalt, fine. Sand, fine. A piece of wood, fine.

When we get tired, we like to close our eyes and go to sleep. Why? Because this is our nature. I have seen it in cockpits, going mach decibel 85 – 85 percent the speed of sound—thundering away. There you are over the North Atlantic where so many airplanes and so many lives have been lost. But I have seen the best of them sitting there—quiet, at 45,000 feet with the engines humming and nobody to talk to—nodding off. I have also seen them wake up after doing that, look around, and pretend they're fine. I don't fault them. I just say, "Why don't you go back and take a nap? Ten minutes, fifteen minutes, you'll be fresh. I'll watch the airplane. No problem."

Through logic, you cannot stop the feeling of wanting to know that which will make you truly content, not fairy-tale content. Because until that happens, you will have everything but satisfaction. You will have everything but peace. You will have everything but love. You will have everything but understanding. And those are the things you need—every day.

When you are hungry, you like to eat. When you are thirsty, you like to drink. It's your nature. Is conquering your nature the solution? No. But that's what a lot of people think: "I will conquer my nature. I will *change* it." No. How could you?

I watched a documentary on TV that said if the creation of Earth happened twenty-four hours ago, human beings have only been on Earth for fifteen seconds. And you want to change? We are a little too young to change. We invented the device called a *chair* probably not even one second ago, and we are already fighting with it. We can't sit too long. Why? Because we have a tailbone at the end of the spine. Why? Because we used to have a tail.

Now we have cell phones, and we think that because we have cell phones, we never had a tail. Ask your chiropractor. Your cell phone has nothing to do with your tail. Your tailbone is still there. We see all these advances, and we get excited: "Oh, we are so different now." No, you're not. What do you talk about on the cell phone? Anything new? Anything different? No. It's always, "Hello? Hello? Hello?!"

Somebody gives us a piece of paper that says, "Now you are Dr. So-and-So or Captain So-and-So." So now we think that's who we are.

In India, I was interviewed on a national TV show. The host said to me, "So who are you? What's your real name?" And I said, "Me." He said, "No, no, no. What's your real name?" I said, "*Me*. Me." He said, "No, no, no. What is written in your passport?"

Here is the analogy I gave: Imagine you're in a house. Everything is fine. Your name is So-and-So. Then there is an earthquake, and the house falls down. Now you are buried in the rubble, but you're alive. You hear a rescue party outside. What are you going to say? "Help Mr. So-and-So"? No. Just, "Help *me*." It's uncanny. All of a sudden, all the names disappear—they don't matter.

FREE TO UNDERSTAND
You may have a place where you stay, but do you think you are free because you can come and go as you like?

Last year, I visited a prison to talk to some of the inmates. It was beautiful. Beautiful people, because they *are* people. They've done something wrong, obviously—that's why they're in prison. But I was not there to judge them. The judge already did that.

I didn't go there to free them from the prison, either. It wasn't a jailbreak. I went there to show them the freedom inside of them because they still had it. The drum of breath was still beating, and they should hear it; they should listen to it, and they should awaken to it. That's how it should be because that's the possibility.

It truly is about knowing the freedom inside. That's real freedom. Freedom to understand.

Are you free to understand? Or are you slave to other people's ideas that prohibit you from understanding anything else? If you're not free to understand, then you're not free.

Are you free to understand? Are you free to know? Are you part of a story, a fairy tale that doesn't exist, or are you part of a story in which there is no limit to appreciation? If you don't know how to cook, then it's all about the cooking. But when you know about cooking, the first thing you understand is it's about how to make the food taste wonderful, how to bring out the flavors of the dish. It's totally different. When you don't know about painting, it's all about painting. But when you know about painting, it's not about painting. It's about something else. It is about the dance of life. It's about the color, the subtlety, how it plays with your eyes: "What can I put on this piece of canvas, and what emotion will it spark?"

When you don't know how to appreciate, then you say, "Oh, appreciate life every day." When you really know about appreciation, it is about enjoying the uniqueness of every moment. Do you know that every moment in your life is unique? You will never have two alike. Never. This is the science of living—when you begin to appreciate every moment. Not sitting there saying, "Oh, there goes a moment, there goes a moment, there goes a moment," but to be ready for the moment before the moment comes. To have a heart so open, an understanding so beautiful, and a yearning for appreciation so complete that when that moment comes, you see exactly what it is. That is the only thing that is real.

Couples always say, "Do you love me?" The protocol is the other person says, "I love you," and you're supposed to say, "I love you, too." At that moment, your mind might be completely filled with something else, but what comes out of your mouth? "Oh, I love you, too." This is the fantasy.

We say, "I love," without understanding. We say, "I understand," without understanding and "I know" without knowing. And the subject of the infinite is dealt with by theories and lectures when it should only be the subject of feeling, not words. You do not need to live in a dream. That's what's beautiful about living. You do not need to take your clues from a dream. You need only to close your eyes so that they can open to the land within.

The infinite is not a topic of conversation. All you can do is feel it. Experience it. And then you will understand.

To rest in the most profound way. To come home for real, not in fantasy. To feel alive, not because somebody gave you permission to, but because you feel alive yourself. Not to borrow somebody else's understanding but for *you* to understand. To understand that this breath is a blessing because you have felt it—not because I said so. This is so beautiful. I know that the words alone are quite nice, but it's not about the words. It's about breaking through the wall of words and into reality.

A DANGEROUS FANTASY

There is a beautiful couplet by Kabir: "That a drop resides in the ocean, everyone knows. But that the ocean resides in a drop, only a few know."

Think about it: That a drop resides in the ocean, everyone knows. But that the ocean resides in the drop, only a very few know. I want you to be the very few who know. Who is the drop? And what is the ocean? You're the drop. Me, you, we're the drops. And within us resides the ocean. Not words. When you can feel that ocean inside of you, you will know and understand. Then it's clear and all is as it should be. You feel alive. You don't have to wait for spring to come. Even in the dead of winter, even in poverty, you feel alive.

Somebody asked me a question: "I'm poor, I'm uneducated, and I am old. Do you think I can feel this peace?" In the fairy tale, if you are poor, you are no one. Who came up with that story? "I'm uneducated. I have no possibilities. And I'm old. I'm weak." When the question was first asked to me, I said, "Sure, you can feel this."

Later, I was thinking more about it: "Oh, my God. This man has been reading the wrong story!"

But do you know what's dangerous? It's the same story that was told to us, too. We fear the same three things this man does. We don't want to get old. We don't want to be perceived as uneducated. We dread being poor. And we thought this man was so different from us? No. He was told the story and he bought it; we were told the same story and we bought it. It's a fantasy.

What hope does a person who lives in prison have? Every day that this person accepts the gift of life, his whole life is filled with hope. It's not about a story. It's about reality. You are not about a story. You are alive. Feel that blessing come in your life. Listen to the drum of that breath and dance to it. Be excited because you're alive today. Inside, understand.

THE SPRING OF LIFE

This is not about conquering frustration. Some people think that if a person has inner peace, you can go right up to them and say, "Your flight is not going to leave," and they're going to stay completely composed. It's not like that. Tell a dog, "Your flight's not going to take off," and what will the dog do? Wag its tail and be perfectly happy. You think that's what it's about? So you can be just like that dog?

That's not the point of existence. Neither is it to become Superman. The point of existence is to view this beautiful painting God has created, called you and me, in the most beautiful way. Only when that is happening in your existence can you even remotely begin to say that you are alive.

The seasons pass through every year. The seasons of life come but once. So spring is going to come in your life but once. Are you going to let that spring bloom? To bloom with certainty, with reality, with opportunity? Not as a thought of tomorrow, but a yearning: "Tomorrow I can be fulfilled again as I am today. As I am now. Not with my faults but with my strength. Not by what I don't know but by what I *do* know."

When people can find that reality within them, joy is the reward. Joy is the gift. So, no fantasy, but a reality. The reality is more beautiful than any imagined fantasy.

"That a drop resides in the ocean, everyone knows. But that the ocean resides in a drop, only a few know."

Think about it.
Me, you, we're the drops.

And within us resides the ocean. Not words.

When you can feel that ocean inside of you, you will know and understand.

There is a voice for peace that sees
no difference between the rich and the poor,
between different types of governments,
between an educated and an uneducated person.

Please, do not squelch that voice.
Assist it, because peace is an innate need
of every person—just like the need
for water and food, for air and shelter.

PART TWO

LISTEN TO THE VOICE FOR PEACE

The answer will not come from a book.
The answer will not come from outside.
The answer will come from within you.

THIS QUEST
IS REAL

For me, if there is any meaning to the word *civilization*, it lies in the understanding that, of all things I do, I do not turn against another human being. Regardless of the reason, regardless of the excuses that countries make, regardless of the ideals of today, civilization, to me, means to be civilized. To be civil.

I talk about the possibility of peace. I am sure some people wonder, "How is peace possible?" Let me make my case: Peace is possible. Because peace begins with every single human being on the face of this earth.

In your eyes, you don't need to greet yourself.

That is why the self is not valued in this world today.

Many people think that peace is the absence of war. I agree and I disagree. Which war are we talking about? The one out there, in the world? Or the one in here, in me? People think that the absence of hunger will bring peace to this earth. Which hunger are we talking about? The one in my stomach? Or the one in my heart? My heart has a hunger, too. I, as a human being, have a quest.

WHAT IS PEACE?

My quest is to be content. And contentment doesn't come from having everything—but that's what so many people think. You see, the problem that I face when I say words like *peace* and *contentment* is that I don't know if we're talking about the same thing, because everybody has their own version.

What is peace? If you want to know the answer to this question, let me suggest something. The answer is not going to come from a book, and it is not going to come from outside. It is going to come from within you. Because within you is the thirst for peace, and within you is the water that will quench that thirst.

You have learned to ask questions. You're brilliant at asking questions; you can ask amazing questions. But are you also brilliant at recognizing the answers? Why do I ask you this? Because, with all the questions that have come from within you, you have always had the answers within you as well. But did you ever look at them? Did you acknowledge them?

YOU DON'T GREET YOURSELF

You acknowledge everybody around you. You acknowledge your friends, your wife, your husband, your sister, your brother, your uncle. When you get up in the morning, your husband or wife may not say, "Hi" or "Hello," but they have a way of looking at each other that means "Hello." You meet your friend, and you say, "Hello." You meet your boss, and you say, "Good morning, sir."

But how do you greet yourself? You don't. You never figured out a way to greet yourself. Because in your eyes, you don't need to greet yourself. That is why the self is not valued in this world today. So many scriptures say that you must understand the

**You have felt many joys.
But there is another joy
that you need to feel:
the joy of being alive.**

self, but people say, "I don't know what that means." When people read scriptures, they don't read the lines anymore. They only read between the lines. If you only read the lines, you don't need any interpretation. If you read between the lines you will, because there's nothing there. And "nothing" needs a lot of interpretation. So, there is no shortage of people who are interpreting.

Can you imagine people doing that with their food? There you are. You are very hungry, and you are waiting to have your food served, and the cook says, "I made amazing things for you. I made you fifty dishes. I made you the best dessert." Your mouth is watering, your stomach is growling, "Food, food, food." So you say, "Great. Bring it!" And the person says, "No, no. Let me first talk to you about it. Let me describe what I made. Let me tell you how wonderful it will be when you taste this dessert."

It wouldn't work for you, would it? Hunger has to be satisfied. Thirst has to be satisfied. Why not the quest of your heart? What is the difference?

You say, "If I don't eat and drink, I will die." I say, "If you don't fulfill the quest of your heart, you *are* dead." And that is why today, human beings don't recognize the value of other human beings. Dead people do not say hello to each other.

What does it mean to you to be alive? I know you have responsibilities. But right now, you think taking care of your responsibilities is the *only* responsibility you have. I say that fulfilling this quest is *also* your responsibility. Many people give this excuse: "If I want to fulfill the quest of my heart, I will have to leave my family. I will have to leave my job. I will have to leave everything I have." Why? Your family is on the outside. Your heart is on the inside.

The day I accepted and understood that I wanted to make the journey toward peace, I took the first step toward getting closer to myself. The truest understanding of the self begins with that first step. To acknowledge the thirst. To acknowledge that the quest you have had your whole life is not a frivolous quest but a real quest that you can fulfill.

What will happen to me, to you? I have no illusions. This body is dirt. Most of the elements that make up this earth are dirt, and one day, the dirt will go back to being dirt.

ARE YOU FREE?
There's a beautiful saying: "When you came into this world, you cried, and the world laughed. Do something so that when you die, you laugh and the world cries." Do something that is real—and there is nothing more real than experiencing the peace that dances inside of you.

70

That peace is not far away. It dances in the hearts of all human beings—waiting, looking to be embraced, to be accepted, to be understood, to be discovered, to be found. By *us*. The expression of that peace brings a smile unparalleled. The expression of that peace dancing on a face makes it look beautiful. The expression of that peace fulfills the desire of the heart.

You think you are free. But are you? Or are you enslaved? Do you think about the things that you want to think about? Or do you think about the things you *don't* want to think about? People get up in the morning, and they start thinking, "Oh, I have to do this, and I have to do that. What's going to happen to my business?" We think we are free. We are not. But I am talking about a freedom, a peace, that people can experience even if they are in prison. I am sure many people wonder, "How is that possible? You can't experience freedom in a prison!" Yes, you can.

When people come to hear me speak, the first thing many of them say is, "Okay, give me the magic formula."

I say, "But I have given you the magic formula. Peace is inside of you."

"So how do I get to it?" they ask.

"If you want to get to it, stop trying, because you already have it."

A REAL THIRST
When you don't know where or what you are looking for, it is only by a divine act of randomness that you will find it, if you are lucky. But if you know that peace is inside of you, stop wasting your time: You won't find it in books. Next time you are hungry or thirsty, read a book. It doesn't work, does it?

When you came into this world, you cried, and the world laughed.

Do something so that, when you die, you laugh and the world cries.

Hunger is real. It requires food—not theory or philosophy. You can read and write as many recipe books as you want, but don't forget to eat. And maybe that is as simple as my message is: Don't forget the real thing in your life. Your time is limited.

You think you're going to live forever, especially when you're young. That is not true. The time comes when everything begins to fade. You don't have the stamina anymore. You don't see as well, so you need glasses. Hearing starts to fade: "Huh?" Maybe all of these things are trying to tell you something. Instead of listening to other people, listen to something within you. Instead of looking at all the other people, like you've been doing all your life, maybe the time has come to look at you. All your life, you've been running, running, running. Going here, going there. When you get old, it becomes a little difficult.

Maybe it's trying to tell you, "Hey. Stop running around. Settle down. And look at the most magnificent thing that is happening to you."

Feel it. Feel the coming and going of this incredible blessing called *breath*. Wonder no more. Understand that the miracle of all miracles is taking place.

Nobody pays attention to this miracle of breath until it is too late. When it starts to leave, then everybody says, "Just one more, and one more, and one more"—until it is no more.

This is a fate we all share. You don't have to make an appointment. It will happen. It is more guaranteed than anything else in your life. And yet, in the moments that you have while you are alive, what is your focus, what is your goal, what is your aim? Which bucket are you filling?

LIGHTING THE WORLD

How much water can you put in a bucket that has a hole in it? If your bucket has a hole in the bottom, you can pour in the water from all the oceans, but it will not hold a single drop. It is doomed to be empty. As soon as that hole was created, whatever water was in the bucket drained out. And from then on, it doesn't matter what you do: It is doomed to be empty.

If you have a hole of confusion, of delusion, of questions and no answers, of anger, of doubt, then your bucket will also remain empty. Don't worry about the water. Worry about plugging up the holes. Because if there are no holes in the bucket, then, believe me, even if you just leave it outside and a little dew falls in, the bucket will hold it. Water will come and fill it. You don't have to worry—if there are no holes.

In this world, I see so many holes, and nobody is filling them. To light a football field takes many lamps, which are actually quite small, but together they can light

Human beings are the lamps of the world. Unless we are lit, there is not going to be light.

the whole field. We human beings are the lamps of this world. And unless we are lit, there is not going to be light. We are the ones who need the light, and when that light in our hearts is lit, then and only then will there be some illumination in this very dark night.

It begins with us. The good news is, what you are looking for is inside of you. The peace you want is within you. I offer a mirror so that you can see yourself—*you*. Not the ideas about you, not how you should be, but how magnificently you have been created.

THE JOURNEY BEGINS

Truly, the journey of a lifetime begins with your heart, with you. That's how simple it is. That's how real it is. And when you take that first step, you feel the joy. You have felt many joys, but there is another joy that you need to feel—not once, but every day of your life. And that is the joy of being alive.

Then a heart full of gratitude says, "Thank you. Thank you for this breath, for this time, for this life, for this fulfillment." Is this possible? Yes, it is. Is it real? Yes, it is. All that is between you and this possibility of peace is a simple veil. When the veil is lifted, you will be able to see, understand, and appreciate the magnificence of life.

I go from place to place and talk about peace. Do I make a difference? I don't know. But something has made a difference in my life, and I will keep trying. Some people ask me, "Is this practical? Can you really do it?" Well, the fulfillment of ambitions doesn't belong to "the practical people." It has always, historically, belonged to those who have tried, because their heart told them to try.

So look for peace. Search for it. Whatever you have to do, find peace in your life. If you don't find it, come look me up. I can help.

Don't forget the real thing in your life.
Your time is limited.

You think you're going to live forever,
especially when you're young.
That is not true.

The time comes when everything begins to fade.
You don't have the stamina anymore.
You don't see as well, so you need glasses.
Hearing starts to fade: "Huh?"

Maybe all of these things are trying
to tell you something.
Instead of listening to other people,
listen to something within you.

Instead of looking at all the other people,
like you've been doing all your life,
maybe the time has come to look at you.

All your life, you've been running.
Going here, going there.
When you get old, it becomes a little difficult.

Maybe it's trying to tell you,
"Hey. Stop running around.
Settle down.
And look at the most magnificent thing
that is happening to you."

Feel the coming and going
of this incredible blessing called *breath*.

Wonder no more.
Understand that the miracle of all miracles
is taking place.

LISTEN TO
THE VOICE

You might find my perspective a little different. I'm not associated with big institutions. When I travel and talk to people, I really talk to *people*. Sometimes we forget that we all are human beings. We get so caught up in our causes, in our definitions of everything, that we forget to look around and see that we—each one of us—are human beings with the same fundamental ambition: to be happy, to be in peace.

A lot of people talk about peace, and sometimes I ask them, "What does peace mean to you?" For many, peace is an absence of something. You go somewhere to get away from the noise of the traffic. Soon you're overlooking a beautiful lake, where everything is very serene, and you say, "Oh, it's so peaceful." Or you might think that if you climb Mt. Everest or accomplish some goal in your life, maybe then you'll be in peace.

THE QUEST

But what *is* peace? What was it like for Socrates or Plato to even contemplate the idea of peace? There weren't tanks or airplanes back then, but people were still trying to cope with problems not so dissimilar to ours.

What was the quest? To bring peace to every individual. So, again, it brings up the question, what is peace? Is it something innate that resides in the heart of every human being? Or is it a state that can be manipulated and brought about from the outside? There is a fundamental difference between these two. When I speak about peace, I say that the desire for peace has resided within human beings since time immemorial and continues today. And there is a voice for peace that surfaces again and again—despite how many times it has been ignored.

It has been ignored by governments and world leaders. We have found ourselves at war again and again. And even in the face of that, the voice for peace continues to call out. We need to acknowledge it. We need to listen to it. This voice doesn't belong to a specific group of people; it doesn't belong to any one country. It is every single human being, in their own way, searching and trying to find peace. That's how powerful it is.

It is the voice that sees no difference between the rich and the poor. It is the voice that sees no difference between different types of governments. It is the voice that sees no difference between an educated person and an uneducated person. Please do not squelch that voice. Assist it, because peace is an innate need of every person—just like the need for water and food, for air and shelter.

REASONS FOR PEACE

People all around the world cry out for peace. I know. I meet with people who are extremely poor and people who are extremely rich. When they begin to express what they need in their lives, it becomes obvious that what each one wants is exactly the same.

Sometimes we see the reasons peace is *not* happening. And we don't realize that peace is not that far away from each one of us.

It is no accident that we find ourselves at unwanted thresholds again and again. When wars are created, people look for *reasons* to justify them. It is time that we start to look for reasons for peace, because that's what has *not* been given a chance.

**What was the quest?
To bring peace
to every individual.**

"I didn't do anything.

All I did was show you who you are."

Nobody wants war. Why? Who does war inflict the most pain on? The innocent. And these innocent people are simple. They did no wrong. Their ambition is to have food. Maybe they can't even dream of having it three times a day, but they hope to have it at least twice a day. They dream of a shelter, a better life for their family, a future for their children. That's all they want. Going into space is optional. They don't think that far.

Not long ago, I was in a taxi, talking with the driver. He was asking, "What's going to happen to our children?" All this man wanted was the opportunity to have peace.

Wherever you turn, wherever you go, this is the fundamental need that people have. Is it that hard? Is it impossible? In times of trouble, what do we need? When we have personal problems, we need strength. And at the end of the day, that strength comes from within you. Other people might be catalysts, but the strength comes from within you.

Peace is no different. The quest for peace comes from within you, and the peace you are looking for is also within you. People say, "So what is the formula?" The formula is obvious.

LION OR LAMB?
Once there was a farmer who came across a lion cub. He saw that the lion cub was ill and very weak, so he brought it back home, gave it milk, and put it in his barn, which was filled with sheep.

So, the cub grew up spending all his time with sheep, until one day he was no longer a cub. He had become a young lion.

One day, while the sheep were grazing, a big lion came out of the jungle and roared. The sheep scattered all over the field trying to hide, and so did the young lion. The

78

big lion saw him and said, "Why are *you* hiding?"

He said, "Well, you're going to eat me."

The big lion said, "No! Don't you know who you are?"

And the little lion said, "I'm a sheep. But whatever you say, I'll agree with it, because I don't want you to eat me."

The big lion said, "No, no, no. Come with me. I want to show you something." He took him to the lake and said, "Take a look."

And when the young lion looked at his reflection in the water, he saw that he was not a sheep. He was indeed a lion. He started thanking the big lion, and the big lion said, "I didn't do anything. All I did was show you who you are."

MORE TO IT

I like that story because sometimes that's what happens to us. We forget our fundamental nature. And when we cannot see who we are, how can we respond to the needs of those around us? It's impossible. We are not what we think we are. We are a precious gift in the midst of this magnificent creation.

Last night, I looked up and saw the beautiful stars. And yet, not long ago, I was watching a TV documentary that showed how violent it is in outer space. Black holes. Planets. Stars. Massive explosions. Standing there last night, it was incredibly serene. How could it be? Is that a mistake? Is it all a mistake? Or is there more to it?

I say there is more to it. There is a want for peace in everyone. The desire for peace dances in the heart of every human being. That is good news. As long as people are on the face of this earth, the need for peace will exist. If we acknowledge this need and seek to fulfill it, we can feel what it is like to be happy.

If you want happiness in your life, you need peace first. Then happiness will follow. That's my personal observation from traveling and talking to people around the world. And I try to make it possible for them to find that peace in their lives.

What I talk about comes from my own experience.
Somebody helped me to discover the river.
And now I have access to the water.

THE RIVER

Once there was a man who bought a house, but there was a shortage of water there. So he did a lot of research, and he found the place where he should dig a well. He bought a spade and started digging. It was hot, and it was hard. And one day, he reached his limit.

He had no more water; he had been working for days in the heat of the sun, digging the well. He was incredibly thirsty, and he knew that if he didn't get water very soon, he would die.

So he started yelling, "Water, water, water." Somebody heard him and came over to him and said, "Come with me. I will take you to the water." The stranger took his hand and led him around the house. Not far away, a huge river was flowing with beautiful clear water.

When the man saw the river, he jumped in. He cooled himself, he drank the water, and he was content. As he came out, he thanked the person, went back to his house, picked up the spade, and continued digging his well.

Why do I tell this story? Because digging the well had become more important than finding the water. The river was not that far from his house. After he found it, he didn't need a well. He could just run a pipe or even fetch the water when he needed some. But he was so involved in digging the well—he had put so much research into it, had spent so much time and energy deciding the exact spot—that even after finding the river, he had to keep digging.

This is what happens to many of us. We get so involved in formulas for how to make everything happen that we actually forget what we are trying to accomplish.

WHO ARE WE?
So, what do you want in your life? What do I want in my life? What do we all want? Who are we? What are we?

As I travel from country to country, I see the signs: "Welcome to India," "Welcome to Malaysia," "Welcome to France." Welcome to all of these places.

Do those nations define who we are? Don't we all descend from those people who knew no nation, who had no sophistication, who only wanted to survive day by day and be content? Are we not a part of those people whose desire was not a cell phone or a computer but existence?

There was a civilization that believed in an afterlife. They built pyramids. Don't you think they looked at those pyramids in bewilderment and pride at the same time? "We did this!" And then, like a book, the page turned, and everything changed. A new chapter began.

So, here we are today. Who are we? What are we? What do we want? Once upon a time, when we were children, the resolve all of us had was to feel joy, to be content. The formulas didn't matter. The ideas didn't matter. The social justifications didn't matter. What mattered was being content. It is so innate. It is so fundamental.

Your life is like a circus that comes to town. It's exciting. They pitch the tents on a field and then create the environment. People buy their tickets, sit down, and watch the show. And one day, the show closes down, and all that is left is the field.

Do the nations define who we are?
Don't we all descend from those people
who knew no nation,
who knew no sophistication,
who only wanted to survive day by day,
and be content?

83

I'm not saying that's good, and I'm not saying that's bad. I pass no judgment on it. It is neither right nor wrong. And I don't tell you how to evade it, because you can't.

JOY
What I am saying is that the circus has come to town, and *you* are the circus. Enjoy. Enjoy this time that you have. Not in the sense of, "Look what I have!" but rather, "Look what I have discovered!" Discover that which already exists inside of you.

What I talk about comes from my own experience. And my experience says that if I have discovered the river, I don't need to dig the well.

I didn't create the river. I didn't even know that there was a river so close. Somebody helped me to discover it, and now I have access to the water.

You ask people, "What is peace?" Some say, "Peace is when all the countries stop fighting." Others tell you, "Peace is when the neighbors don't make noise anymore." Or, "Peace is early morning when nobody else is up, the birds are starting to sing, and the sun is rising."

Let me tell you about a peace that is not bound by definitions. Let me tell you about a peace that is the same for every person on the face of this earth. That peace is not out there.

Ask people, "What is your definition of joy?" Some will tell you, "Joy is winning the lottery." Others will tell you, "Joy is passing the exam that I didn't study for."

An amazing thing happens. Exam time comes, and suddenly everybody, at the last minute, is interested in studying. Actually, they're really not interested in studying; they're interested in passing the exam. And as soon as they pass the exam, they can forget everything they have studied.

The world teaches us about our differences.

But we also have a similarity: the thirst of the heart that every one of us has.

84

KNOW YOURSELF

It was like that for me when I went to school. What was my favorite thing to do? Play, play, play. What was my mother's favorite thing for me to do? Study, study, study. And the more she said, "Study," the more I wanted to play. Then when exam time came, her question was, "Will you pass? Will you pass? Will you pass?"

Let me tell you about the joy that is the same for everybody. The real joy is not about accomplishments. The real joy is not what mountain you have climbed. The real joy is discovering the peace that is within your own self. To find the river in you.

Now, people listen to this and say, "Hmm. How? I don't think there is anything inside of me—it's all outside." What about those people through the centuries who have been saying, "What you are looking for is inside of you"? What about those people who have been saying, "Know thyself"? Or the Chinese proverb I just saw when I was in Taiwan looking through a book: "It is intelligent to know your friends. It is wise to know yourself." I liked it.

Am I saying something that you don't already know? Big question. Have I said something so far—besides the story and the little proverb—that you didn't already know? Each year, hundreds of thousands of people come to hear me speak, and I tell them what they already know. And do you know what's really nice? They like it.

We need to be reminded about the fundamental things that we know. We need to be reminded again and again and again what is important. We forget. And what do we forget? We forget the most important things.

When people travel—and I see this all the time—they don't forget the useless things. Never. They've got those with them. But things like their passport? Missing. You see them at the airport looking for their passport and pulling out all their luggage, going through everything.

In this life, too, we forget our passport. The call of the heart, we forget. We forget because there are calls from everybody else screaming in our ears, "This is what's important; that is what's important." There was a time in your life when the only thing that was important to you was what you felt from within. Your mother said to you, "Be quiet." Were you? "Waaahhh." Your father said, "Shhh!" You still cried. You cried because you had a need. And when that need was fulfilled, you were fine.

THE SIMILARITY

Now, we have grown up. The world has changed; technology has changed. So we think we have changed, too. We fly in jet aircrafts, guided by the most incredibly modern global positioning system with three digital autopilots. So we have changed. Right? Not when we hit the first bump. Try telling yourself, "But you are the modern man. You are the modern woman. Fear not—three digital autopilots. Fear not—global

positioning system. Let go of the chair. It is nothing." Ha-ha. The pilot is doing exactly the same thing in the cockpit. He's got the yoke. He's turned pale. His knuckles are white. He's saying, "Agghghh!"

There's nothing modern about us. We pick up the cell phone and react to the conversation the same way we would if the person were standing in front of us. What a façade has been created, in the belief that we have changed. We have not changed.

Who are we? The world teaches us about our differences. But we also have a similarity. What is it? The similarity is the thirst of the heart that *every one of us* has.

The similarity is the coming and going of the breath. It is the same for every single person alive. It comes, and it brings life. It brings existence. And it goes, and it comes again. And in it is immeasurable joy. Immeasurable peace. Immeasurable satisfaction. Immeasurable tranquility. That is what is dancing on the stage of your heart.

Peace is looking for you. Are you looking for peace? Peace doesn't come about because some leaders get up and say, "Peace, peace, peace." Never. If we want peace, it doesn't begin with the world; it begins with us. I have traveled around the world many times, but I have never come across anything called the *world*. I have come across *people*. People, people, and more people. This is who we are.

Peace is looking for you ...

86

You want to hear about a miracle? You are a miracle. You are this moving, dancing miracle of all miracles. The breath comes into you. Do you know from where? It's the kiss of the creator touching you, bringing you life. Do you know what life is? The very magic that allows you to see, to hear, to feel, to think, to smile, to be, to feel happiness, to feel joy, to feel peace—that is what life is.

The breath comes into you. It allows you to exist, so all these beautiful things can unfold for you. It's yours. And no one can come and steal it away from you.

IT'S NOT SELFISH
Some people say, "Isn't that selfish?" Is enjoying a sunrise selfish? Is happiness selfish? When the little baby smiles, is that selfish? Which grandmother, which mother, thinks it's selfish when her little baby comes waddling up to her to give her a big hug and a sloppy kiss? What father thinks that is selfish? That's not selfish.

You hug that baby. You don't say, "Go hug somebody else." No. It's quite the reverse. When that baby comes and hugs like that, the grandmother is on top of the universe. "Ah, he kissed me. He came to *me*!"

... Are you looking for peace?

87

The breath comes into you.

It's the kiss of the creator, touching you, bringing you life.

It's the same way. This breath came into me. It came and touched *me*. And I hug it back. I embrace it back. And I feel gratitude. What is gratitude? People don't know what gratitude is.

Gratitude is a feeling. When the heart is full, there is gratitude. Allow yourself to be filled with gratitude. Allow yourself to feel peace.

I offer a way to be able to go inside and feel the feeling that is within. People sometimes say, "Give it to me." Give you what? What you already have? What I am talking about is discovery. Open. Open what you haven't opened for a long time. Discover what you haven't discovered for a long time. It doesn't matter how young you are, and it doesn't matter how old you are. The time has come to open the greatest gift of all.

I have met so many people who say: "Life is terrible. You come into this world, you have a horrible experience, and then you die. And that's it." I'm not arguing with them. I don't need to. I don't want to. Maybe this is all they have seen. Maybe bitterness is all they know. They're digging the well, and they are hot. And all I am saying is, there is a river in their backyard.

Some people say, "River or no river, I'm going to dig this well, because I've done the research, and I have already spent all this time. Won't I look like an idiot if I stop digging now?" No, you won't. You will look like the smartest person, the one who found the river and realized, "There's no reason for me to dig the well."

So, this is my message: There is a wonderful possibility within you. Not in a book. Not in a building. Not on top of a mountain. Within you. In your life, in your existence, there is a beautiful possibility. Discover that possibility and be fulfilled. Enjoy this existence. Enjoy each kiss from the creator that comes and touches you.

No kiss is more precious than that kiss.

IN YOU IS
A TREASURE

There was a man who was very poor. He wanted to buy a little farm and saved up as much money as he could. There was some land that nobody was using, so he went to the owner and asked, "Can I buy this farm from you?" The owner said, "Okay, you can have it." He took the money and sold him his farm.

The man worked really hard plowing the fields, and the land yielded beautiful crops. Slowly but surely, he became quite rich. He built himself a house, married, and had children. With most of his wealth, he bought gold. Then he put the gold in a trunk, and he buried the trunk on his land.

Time passed. The man got very old. He called his children to his bedside and said, "It's time for me to go. But please take care of the farm. Plow the fields." He didn't tell them that he had buried the treasure. He just said, "Plow the fields, and you will be rewarded beyond belief."

When he passed away, his children had a cremation ceremony . . . and then they lost all interest in the farm. Once again, it became unused land. One day, somebody came along and said, "Here is a little money. Would you please sell me your farm?" The sons weren't interested in the farm, so they sold it to him.

This man plowed the fields. One day while he was plowing, what do you suppose he came across? The buried treasure. Instantly, he was richer than he could have ever imagined.

THE BEAUTY IN YOU

That treasure is a metaphor for the peace that we are all seeking. I want to talk about this peace. I don't want to tell you what is right and what is wrong. I'm not trying to point out all the problems of the world, because there are too many. But, despite all those problems, despite all the things that are wrong in this world, there are some things that are really, really good. Despite all the ugliness in this world, there is something very, very beautiful. Despite all the mistakes that have been made, there is something that is perfect. And that perfection, that beauty, is in you. That is what I want to talk about.

There are people who like to point out all the problems. And, in a way, I'm glad they do. But I think there should also be people who point out the good, the right, the beautiful, because this existence that you have is beautiful, is wonderful. And sometimes, caught up in our troubles, in our turmoil, in our ideas, we forget the importance of being alive.

You look at the desert, and it's so dry, but the time to see the desert is not in the summer. It is when it rains, because mysteriously even the desert holds within it the promise of beautiful life, of delicate, tender flowers. But it needs the rain. The water has come before in that desert and carved the shape of the riverbed. And that dry river waits and waits, patiently, for it to rain and for the water to flow through it once again. It is ready.

YOU!

Who are we? What are we? Are we the sum of all the things that happen around us? Or is there something more than waking up in the morning and realizing one's responsibilities: "I have to do this. I have to do that"? Is there something inside each human being that wants to smile, that wants to be thankful, that wants to feel gratitude and joy?

90

You know a lot about other people, but you know very little about yourself.

I speak from my own experience. I have responsibilities. There are good days. There are bad days. In the good days, I want to be happy. I want to feel peace. I want to feel connected to myself. I want to feel centered. I want to feel like one person, not split into two, three, four, or five. And then there are bad days. And you know what? Even in the bad days, I want to be happy.

I do not want to try to explain the concept of happiness. Nobody can explain it. But many people think that happiness is feeling happy *about* something. Your child graduates from college: "I am so happy." You win the lottery: "I am so happy." You get a promotion: "I am so happy." We think our happiness is associated with all the things in this world, that somehow they are going to make us happy.

But there is only one person in the whole world who can make you happy. Do you know who that is? It happens to be a person that you know very little about. Strange. This person who can make you happy, really happy, you don't know much about. You know a lot about your friends. You know a lot about other people, but you know very little about yourself, who you are. And you are the only person who can make you very happy.

Who are you? You were born. You were given the gift of breath. You don't think much about it. You will, but it'll be at the end of your life when it's getting hard to breathe. Then it will be breath, breath, breath. I see people driving on the highways, honking their horns, yelling, screaming. Somehow, I get the feeling that these people don't really think life is important. They just want to get to where they're going. That's what's important to them. I ask you to take a little time and understand that your life is incredibly important.

You're not a number. You're not a name. I always find it curious when I travel to a country and I have to show my passport. And they ask, "Who are you?" I just want to answer, "I'm me." Because I am more than the picture in the passport. I'm alive. I'm real. But, no, I need a piece of paper to prove I am me. Some countries even issue an identity card. Your picture is on it, but that's not the important part. Your name is on it, but that's not the important part. The important part is that there is a signature from somebody whom you have never met and whom you probably will never meet. This signature verifies that you are you. I know this person didn't even sign it—a machine did. It's just a copy of his or her signature.

I'm not criticizing identity cards and passports. We need those things. But you are more than that piece of plastic. You are more than the sum of all your goods and all your bads. You are more. So many people in this world live in fear. In certain places, it's probably a good idea. But there is a place inside of you that cannot have fear, because in this place you should be feeling freedom. I have a definition of freedom, and it comes from my experience: When somebody has to tell me I am free, then I'm not free.

We have formulas for freedom and formulas for happiness. But happiness has nothing to do with formulas. "This plus this, plus this, equals happiness." No. Either you feel happiness or you don't. Either you feel joy or you don't. Either you feel free or you don't. Either you feel peace or you don't.

Your life is the stage where peace will dance, where happiness will sing a song for you. This is what it is all about. The greatest achievement of man isn't going to the moon. That will be overshadowed by somebody going to Mars. And that will be overshadowed by somebody going even farther out, because somebody will always come along and break the record.

There will be technology in the future that'll be so incredible that they're going to look at us and laugh. They're going to say, "They flew in those things that made noise and belched out smoke. They used to fight about them, because every time one of them would fly overhead, they would make so much noise that people couldn't sleep. So they had to have curfews for them. And they had freeways. There were traffic jams and accidents. And everybody carried these little things that beeped all the time. It got so bad that they had to write etiquette for them: 'You must turn these off when you are at a restaurant or in public places like the library.'" They will laugh at us, just as we laugh at the people before us. That's the game of this world.

You build a house and say, "This is my home." Does the home say, "You are my owner"? After you are gone, somebody else will move in, and they will call it their home. And after they're gone, somebody else will call it their home.

What is yours? Do you know? This breath pounding into you—where does it come from? Where does it go? Every time it comes, it brings the gift of life. What is life? When you are conscious, this life holds promise after promise after promise for you, gift after gift after gift. Which gift have you accepted? If you are a stranger to your own self, then you came, you lived a while, and then you were gone.

You don't even have to make an appointment. It's going to happen. You have no control over it. But between birth and death, I can do something. Of all the things I can accomplish, let it be that I am fulfilled, that I know my self. And let it be that of all the people I have tried to understand, I understand myself. Because this world is a desert, and I want the rain of peace and understanding to come. There are dry rivers here waiting to flow again. There are seeds that are waiting to sprout, to blossom.

SPRING HAS COME

It is so beautiful to watch spring come. Right outside my office in my home, there is a tree. Last winter, it shed every leaf, leaving only bare branches. Then slowly but surely, spring began to come. Not a day was wasted for those green shoots to start appearing. This I call *dedication*. This I call *devotion*. This I call *life*. This I call the *grand miracle*. But if that tree were human, it would say, "Why are we doing this? Winter's going to come again, and then I'm going to have to shed these leaves again. So forget about blooming; just hibernate."

No. It is not logical. It is something that transcends logic. Love is not logical. But even though it is not logical, it doesn't lose its importance. These little shoots wait and wait, and in that waiting, they cannot forecast the weather. They don't say, "Hey, I know these two days are warm, but then the next two days it's going to be raining again, so just wait." No, no, no. Instead they say, "Here it is. The warmth has come. The sun is shining. The temperature is right. Let's go." As tender and delicate as those shoots are, even with the two days of cold and rain, they say, "We will bear it and keep going, keep going, keep going." They take a chance, a calculated risk. This scene plays out for thousands upon millions upon billions of trees and branches on the face of this earth every year.

For you, too, spring has come. It is time to reach within and let the hope for peace resurface in your life, to see the good, to understand the good, to know once again and say yes to what you have ignored for so long, which is no one else but you! Because in you is a treasure. And like the man who plowed the fields, you can find that treasure.

**If you are a stranger
to your own self,
then you came,
you lived a while,
and then you were gone.**

93

WHAT MAKES YOU HAPPY?

Let me begin with a question: What makes a cow happy? I've been around cows, and I can tell you one thing. What makes a cow happy is just being a cow. When is an alligator happy? When it is being an alligator. You could take an alligator and put a diamond-studded chain on its neck, try to put lipstick on it, tie it to a very expensive chair that used to be Napoleon's, and say, "You look beautiful. The lipstick really brings out your lips, and you're sitting in Napoleon's chair." But the alligator doesn't really care about those things. It just wants to be an alligator and do its alligator thing—whatever that is.

I talk about a reality that is so incredibly real that it is beautiful. I talk about a joy that is so real that it is not connected to yesterday or tomorrow. It is only in the present, in this moment called *now*. I talk about a happiness that is *your* happiness—not dependent on anybody else or on any circumstance or any situation, but just on you.

I talk about a wealth that you have, a wealth that is priceless. You cannot sell it, and you cannot buy it. Because you have it, you are the wealthiest person on the face of this earth. What is it?

WHAT MAKES YOU HAPPY?

A cow being a cow is happy; a dog being a dog is happy; a cat being a cat is happy; and an alligator being an alligator is happy. So the question is, what makes *you* happy? You have probably seen those commercials where people are sitting on the beach, drinking beer, roasting some poor animal on the fire, and saying, "It doesn't get any better than this." I disagree, but this is what they want you to think. Before you answer the question of what makes you happy, keep one thing in mind. The alligator was not dependent on anything else—just being itself was what made it happy. For the cat, it was just being a cat.

It would be a sad day if your happiness depended on someone else or something else. Then your life would not be dedicated to enjoying happiness, but to being around the person who makes you happy or preserving the situation that makes you happy.

That might answer some of the questions people have about what we are doing in this world. We try to preserve all that we like and think is good. The whole world is busy trying to do just that. Nobody's enjoying themselves because enjoyment is not important. What has become important is making sure that those circumstances and those people are there.

How many parents whose children have grown up wish they could all come together the same way they did when they sat around the table laughing and having a wonderful meal? How many parents try to re-create that again and again unsuccessfully? It's only the parents who are into it—not the kids. The kids are saying, "Give me a break. I have my own life; I want to do my thing." And the parents say, "No, no, no. We're going to re-create that exact scene. Weren't we all having a good time? Let's do that again." Pictures on the wall.

Can true joy be dependent on anyone else? We are talking about the truest of all joys. The truest reality. Is it harsh? Or is it sweet? For those who have felt it, the truest reality is the sweetest reality. It's a reality that says, "I exist. I am alive. The most beautiful gift, the most incredible wealth of the breath is being given to me, and I am conscious. I am aware. I have the capacity to understand. Not only do I have a yearning to be happy, but I also have the source of happiness within me."

FOOD AND HUNGER

We sometimes forget that both things are important—having the yearning to be happy, to be in peace and having the source of happiness and peace inside of us. If you have food but don't have hunger, having the food is like, "Hmm. Wait." But when you have hunger *and* you have food, you say, "Ah. That's good."

A lot of people ask me, "So how do we get to it? Where is it?"

I tell them that peace isn't the problem. Peace is inside of you. The problem is the yearning, the hunger. Standing in the middle of a field where vegetables and fruit are growing, the issue isn't food. The issue is hunger.

You are looking at tomatoes, but not the same way a hungry person does. The hungry person says, "Tomatoes!" while the person who isn't hungry asks, "What kind are they? Do you think they're a bit green? Can I touch one?" It's a different mindset.

Why do I use the word *hunger*? Why don't I use the word *need*? Let me draw a distinction. Somebody can actually make me feel like I need something when I don't, but if I am not hungry, nobody can make me hungry. Hunger is something I have to feel and know.

Some people are more interested in asking, "Where do I get peace?" It is within you! And I'm not the first one to say that. Hundreds and hundreds before me have said, "Peace is inside of you. Peace is possible." The problem isn't peace. The problem is, are we feeling the hunger for peace?

Why do I use the word *thirst*? Nobody can create it for me. Either I am thirsty or I am not thirsty. Somebody can tell you that you are not really thirsty. But you know when you are and when you are not.

TRUE REALITY

Some things are so innate to us, they are not influenced by other things. The issue is your desire for peace, for that reality, for that joy. Unbiased. Because the true reality is not whether you are rich or poor. The true reality isn't whether you are healthy or sick. That can change in a day. You can show up at the doctor's office, and the doctor tells you, "You're going to die." The next doctor says, "Oops. Wrong medical result. You're going to live. It's okay." One day, you were thinking, "Oh, my God! I'm going to die." The next day, "I'm okay, I'm healthy."

We have seen that with the business of being rich or poor. A person is really rich, and the next thing you know, it's all gone. "Oops." That's not the reality.

What is the reality? That you are alive! Somebody might be thinking, "What kind of reality is that?" It's the only kind. It allows you to be rich and allows you to be poor.

You have a wealth that is priceless. You cannot sell it, and you cannot buy it.

Because you have it, you are the wealthiest person. What is it?

Allows you to shed a few tears and allows you to crack a smile. Allows you to dance and allows you to sit still. Allows you to be an uncle, a mother, a dad, an aunt. Without that reality, there is no show.

Reality is simple. What is unfolding every day is not your life. It's the drama in your life. You really have to understand this. What is changing is not the book; it's the pages that are being flipped.

You came into this world, and you will come into this world but once. How absolute is that? Extremely. And it's happened. It has taken place. That's when the book opened. Now the pages are being flipped, and you're reading. And what is on the page? Some of it is your wants, your wishes.

Everybody has a desire of some sort, somewhere, buried. There are some who wish they were taller, while the ones who keep banging their heads against everything wish they weren't so tall. Those who are overweight wish they weren't overweight. Everybody wishes they were better looking. Some people wish they were born to rich parents so they could do anything they want.

Everybody has a little wish, a little desire. We try to make sense out of why things aren't the way we want them to be. Some people turn to the stars—literally. "Pluto was here, Uranus was there, so that's why today is not your day."

DEPENDENT ON WHAT?
And then there are people who are very scientific about it. They say, "I'm a self-made person." Not really; your parents made a contribution! Once I was driving somewhere, and the person I was with said, "So-and-so has finally come to hear you. They never wanted to before because they felt they were self-made and they didn't need help from other people."

I said, "Oh, so they were dependent on that—that they don't need help from other people." But you still need the help from the farmer to grow the vegetables and the grocer to make sure that they are available to you. You still depend on the person who cooks. Or, if you cook yourself, you depend on utensils and the fire. You depend on water coming out of the faucet and all the people who make it possible at the waterworks department. You depend on the pilots who take you where *you* want to go—not where they want to go.

We'd like to think we're independent, when we actually depend so much on so many. That's not the issue here, though. The issue is, in your independence, are you dependent on you or not? It's a tricky question. How can I depend upon myself if I don't even know who I am?

WHEN I AM JUST ME
An alligator knows who an alligator is. A cat knows who a cat is. A dog knows it's a dog. The human being, with the biggest brain for the body size, thinks, "Hmm. Who *am* I? Who am I?" With the run of the earth and the surface of the ocean, the human being asks, "Why am I here? What am I doing here? "

Maybe I will be the happiest if I can be just me. If I only *knew* who I was. Who am I? Things change. I remember a time in my life when I was very young. I didn't go to school. Play, play, play. I was the youngest, and I would get up *really* early in the morning. I couldn't wait to get up. I would be lying there, looking at the window to see the first tinge of light so I could dash outside. I used to watch in incredible amazement how the dew was changing colors, sparkling like diamonds when the sun's first rays hit it.

When I was put in kindergarten, I remember I was crying and crying. My home was better. And then I got used to it. See the change? I actually got used to it. And I traded getting up in the morning and watching the dew for kindergarten.

Then I was enrolled in school, at St. Joseph's Academy. And again I remember

98

For those who have felt it, the truest reality is the sweetest reality.

It's a reality that says, "I exist. I am alive."

crying. I didn't want to go there. It was new; it was different. All my friends were back in kindergarten. And I exchanged kindergarten for St. Joseph's. Things kept changing. I kept exchanging. Changing/exchanging. Changing/exchanging.

In some of that, there were things that were not good, and they went. And there were things that were superb, and they went, too. Indiscriminate throwing out of stuff. And the only thing that has remained constant has been the coming and going of breath. And the desire to be fulfilled.

WHERE IS HEAVEN?
Even when I am fulfilled, the desire to be fulfilled grows greater. It's like love. When you don't love, there is no love. When you love, you love even more. Then you can love even more, and more, and more.

A lot of people think their objective in life is to be fulfilled so that they won't have the desire to be fulfilled. That would be a sad day. When you fall in love with someone, you don't fall in love so that you can stop loving, do you? You fall in love so you can love even more. So you can feel that love more and more. And that has remained constant for me.

When I was growing up, I was the youngest. Now I'm grown up. The only thing that has been constant is this breath that keeps coming. It's a gift. And I accept that, and I understand.

It is true that I'm happiest when I am me. When I am who I am—someone who breathes and feels gratitude in my heart for being alive, a thankfulness that I am alive.

There are people who are so busy trying to figure out what's going to happen to them when they are not alive anymore that they have forgotten how to live. They are so preoccupied with the heaven after death that they have forgotten the heaven on Earth. Voluntarily, they have walked out of the Pearly Gates.

There is a heaven on Earth, and you are equipped to take full advantage of it. Where is this heaven? It's not in some building. This heaven is in the heart of every single human being. The power that created us and knew us so well must have thought: "If I create a heaven that's a physical place, I know these guys will forget how to get there. They'll misplace the address and get lost. I know what I will do. I'll place heaven within them. So wherever they go, one thing they can't do is get lost."

AWAKEN THE THIRST
Wherever I go, I say to people, "What you need is peace," and they understand. When I say *life*, people understand. When I say *breath*, people understand. The value for people to recognize and understand the preciousness of this gift, of this wealth, is the same—whether they're in Japan, in Africa, in India, or in Australia. There

100

are some things that are innate to all of us. We may look different, but we're not. We may talk different, but we're not.

I talk about the possibility of knowing. Knowing *you*. So that you can *be* you. Because without knowing you, you cannot be you, and if you cannot be you, you cannot be happy like the cat, and the crocodile, and the cow. It's important for you to know yourself so that you can be as happy as you can be.

This is how simple it is. I know some of you probably wanted to hear the most sophisticated, mind-boggling thing there is. I'm sorry. It's simple. What you are looking for is within you. And that's not the issue. The issue is the thirst. The issue is the hunger. The day you awaken that hunger inside you, you will find what you're looking for.

Maybe you pull into a gas station and ask the attendant, "Where is Rose Avenue?" If I was the attendant, I would ask you, "Where do you want to go?" You say, "No, no. Tell me where Rose Avenue is."

There is a heaven on Earth, and you are equipped to take full advantage of it.

This heaven is in the heart of every single human being.

When you can experience that joy in your life, when you can understand the value of breath, you have truly begun to understand what life is. Right now, you understand your responsibilities, your chores, your duties. You don't understand life. And believe me, this world needs to understand what life is all about. So much energy is spent just to destroy. Destroy, destroy, destroy. There is so little that brings peace to people. I say, "No. Where do you want to go?"

And you say, "I want to go to the flower shop on Rose Avenue."

And then I will tell you, "There is no flower shop on Rose Avenue. It's on Rose Street."

Do you want to go to the flower shop? Or to Rose Avenue?

This actually happened to me one time, in reverse. I went to a place where I was going to speak, and there was an avenue and a street of the same name. The address on the invitation cards was the avenue, and where they really wanted you to go was the street.

But regardless of that, where do you want to go? People tell me, "I'm looking for this, and I'm looking for that." And I say, "Where do you want to go? I am familiar with this area—just tell me where you want to go, and I'll give you very simple directions to get there."

Too many people are caught up in the logistics of street names. They argue and fight with each other. "No, it's not Avenue. It's Boulevard." Have they ever traversed those streets? Not a footprint. Nobody has walked on those boulevards since the day the cement was laid down. The arguments are about the street names. Somehow, the destination has been forgotten, and street names have become important. In the world of the heart, in the world of this inner scape, destinations are important, not street names.

Awaken in you, then, the thirst to be fulfilled. When the thirst to be fulfilled is awakened in you, you will find your destination.

There is a saying: "Where there is a will, there is a way." The problem isn't the way; it's the will. Some people say, "I'm looking for God. I want to see God." What God? With a beard? Eyes? Light? Void? A few particles? Planet? Palm tree? Mango tree? What? The god you're looking for is in all those things. And what does that which is in everything look like? Have you wondered?

If you are clear about what you want, the best place to look for it is in you, not somewhere out there, because what you're looking for is within you.

YOU CAN KNOW

What is the way? Not the problem. Ignite the thirst. Ignite the hunger for knowledge, for understanding. Don't become a parrot: "Polly want a cracker. Polly want a cracker." Polly does not understand what Polly is, and Polly doesn't have any idea what a cracker is.

Know. Do not repeat—know. Understand. That's your potential. That's one thing you can do. You can know. And you should know. You should be clear. This is your potential—to be clear.

Some people are going to say, "I've heard this before." Good. You obviously didn't pay attention. You're hearing it again. Other people will say, "I've never heard this before." Good! You finally heard it. So pay attention. And fulfill your possibility. Find out who you are so you can be who you are.

Whenever, wherever, even in the darkest hours of pain and suffering, be who you are so you can be happy. So you can be content. So you can find peace in this life. That is important.

There are many, many important things that you have to do. Place this one at the top, and then all that needs to fall into place will fall into place.

When the thirst to be fulfilled is awakened in you, you will find your destination.

You cannot explain what life means.
You need to feel it.

You cannot explain your breath.
You need to breathe it.

You cannot explain what existence means.
It can only be felt.

If you understand that,
an entirely different door opens up to you.

You begin to understand by feeling
—not through explanations.

PART THREE

DON'T EXPLAIN IT
FEEL IT

BELIEVING, REASONING —OR KNOWING

A long time ago, our ancestors lived in trees. They were afraid of all the animals that wanted to eat them. So they'd climb up a tree. It was uncomfortable, but if somebody tried to explain to them that changes are good, they'd say, "No, no, no. You have to start your day alive, and hopefully, when you go to sleep, you'll still be alive, and when you wake up in the morning again, you'll still be alive. That is good."

It must have been terrifying. But slowly they made a change by going into the caves. And from then on, a lot of changes have taken place.

The way we think has been the fastest to change. The human body has not adapted as quickly as the mind has. It's hard to believe, but our eyes actually don't always see in color. Our peripheral vision is in black and white, likely for faster image processing. If something enters your peripheral vision, you can detect it quicker in black and white. In the days when a person might have caught sight of a tiger or a lion leaping out, they didn't care about its color; they didn't care about its stripes. Today you do because most likely you're going to be there with a camera. Just a few years ago, it would have been a gun.

REASONING AND BELIEVING

If you were a caveman, and you heard a mobile phone's ring tone, you'd be terrified, because you'd think it was a new monster, a new animal that was going to eat you. And it was not that long ago that we lived in caves. But the way we think has evolved.

Today we have become very good at reasoning. We reason, and we believe. There was a time when things had to be factual. The knowing had to be very real. It couldn't just be a belief—you had to know. Now we have traded knowing for believing.

Here is an example. You have invited two friends over. One of them has arrived and the other one hasn't, so you ask the friend who has arrived, "Do you think so-and-so will come?" And he says, "I believe"—and the key word is *believe*—"that he will be here shortly." When you ask him why he thinks so, he says, "Because"—and here is the *reasoning* behind the belief—"he is always on time."

This reasoning is flawed. It doesn't take into account that the friend might have had an accident, and no matter how meticulous he is about being on time, he's not going to show up.

Or, let's say you're driving along, and somebody asks you, "Do you think you have enough gas to get where you're going?" and you say, "I believe so." What is it based on? "Well, I know that my destination is fifty miles away, and I still have a half tank of gas. I know that with a full tank of gas, I can go two hundred miles, so I still have plenty of gas." Right? No. This reasoning doesn't take into account that you could get lost in the next fifty miles. In some places, the exits on the motorway are few and far between, so once you get on the wrong highway, that's it.

We have our beliefs, and we have our reasoning. And this, for the most part, seems to suffice. So, to the often-asked question, "Do you believe in God?" many people reply, "Oh, yes. I believe in God." They are told that the stars, the moon, the sun, and the earth are the proof that God exists. This means they have reasoned that there *must* be a God.

A lot of times when people are in trouble, when things are not going their way, they wonder why, like when they get a flat tire and don't know if there is a spare tire in the car. Then when they dig through the trunk, and sure enough, there is a tire, they say, "There is a God after all!" because things just went their way. When they got the flat tire, they didn't say, "Wow! There is a God after all—I have a flat." No. They probably said something totally inappropriate.

The world will have you *believe*. The world will have you *reason*. But some things you have to know.

There is a big difference between reasoning and believing—and knowing. Remember when you were little and you were fascinated by airplanes? You would run around your house, extending your arms for wings, saying, "Wheee!" as you turned. You weren't able to just jump on an airplane, so you pretended, because that was all that was available to you.

But if you come across a pilot who has an aircraft, he could say, "Let's go flying." Then you don't have to pretend. You don't have to hold out your arms. You don't have to believe. You don't have to just reason. You can know.

The world will have you believe. The world will have you reason. But some things you have to know.

WALKING ON COALS
Now the question is, what do you choose to do in your life? Being unconscious is a choice. And being conscious is a choice. Being unconscious seems the easy way. You think that being unconscious conserves energy, but it doesn't. When the consequences strike, it takes a tremendous amount of energy to deal with them.

What is the consequence of unconsciousness? Pain and suffering. If you have ever suffered, you know how much energy it takes. First, you can't sleep. And then it costs a tremendous amount of money. You have to buy tissues; you have to buy books; you have to make phone calls. You have to try to find some relief from this stupid, agonizing suffering. And any relief will do. That's the consequence of unconsciousness.

It might seem like consciousness would take more energy, but it actually doesn't.

109

It saves you on tissues, on books, on all those phone calls—because you're happy. Happiness doesn't cost anything. Everything about happiness is free. When you're happy, you don't think, "Do I have to call somebody? Do I have to do this? Do I have to do that? Do I have to cry? Do I have to read a book about it?" No, you just relax. Everything is wonderful.

Unconsciousness is not economical at all. It costs you time, and it costs you money. You have to go on vacations to try to get away from where you are. Your body is telling you, "This doesn't feel right. What you are doing is not right." It screams. It's called *stress*. And what are the consequences of stress? Ask a doctor. And what does society say? "Let's teach you how to handle stress."

These, by the way, are the same kind of people who would teach you how to walk on coals. Back in the '90s, this was big. People used to have seminars where you learned how to control all these things, and as the last step, you would walk on coals. Now, where would you need to walk on coals? The only place where this could be even remotely useful is in Argentina, where they have huge barbecue pits. They're on the ground, and people have long paddles to handle the food. So if these guys could walk on coals, I guess it could make their job easier.

This is what reasoning does. It tells you that you have conquered something, because you have walked on coals. And if you look back at the whole chain of unconsciousness that led you to walk on coals, how many reasoning links will you find? This is not a small chain. You have believed and believed. And believed some more. And reasoned. And reasoned some more. Till you reached the point where, even if you wanted to get rid of this chain, it is so wrapped around you that your hands literally aren't free to start cutting the links.

And to make matters worse, you want to be free, but you have forgotten what it *feels* like to be free. You want to understand, but you have forgotten *how* to understand, so what happens? Confusion.

KNOWING OR BELIEVING
There is no confusion in knowing. I started speaking to people publicly when I was very young. A man who was in the army heard about me somehow, and he wanted to come and see me, but he was still wondering, "What is a little kid going to teach me? Maybe I will teach him a thing or two."

So he came to my house in India. I was doing homework, and some other people were sitting on the veranda with him. I could hear everybody talking from where I was. The man from the army was having a great time arguing with them, because they were all, in their own way, intellectuals who had abandoned know-how for reasoning. When you know something, there is no argument. But when there is reasoning and belief, there's plenty of room for argument.

110

You want to be free, but you have forgotten what it feels like to be free.

After they argued for a while, someone came to me and said, "There's someone here who came to see you." So I got permission to stop doing my homework, and I went into the living room. The veranda was right outside the living room, which had two sets of doors—one glass and one screen. I opened the glass doors, and as I was listening through the screen, I heard the man saying, "You know, every day I pray to the light." And all this argument was going on, so I sneaked out and sat down quietly. He looked at me, and I looked at him.

And I said, "So, what do you do?"

"Oh, I pray. I pray to the light."

I said, "Oh, that's good. I'm sure that there's no harm in praying to the light, but surely there is no harm in seeing it, either—is there? Have you seen it, too? Or do you just keep praying?" That changed his life.

"Praying to the light" is like knocking on a door. It's not opening, but you keep knocking. The knocking becomes a ritual. What will you do if somebody actually opens the door? You won't know what to do with yourself, because nobody has told you about anything besides the door. You are stuck in the realm of knocking.

DANTE'S HELL
In the fourteenth century, a pope sends Dante into exile. Dante doesn't like that. He sits down and writes a book, *The Divine Comedy*, describing hell. He really gets into it. It's cold, and it's horrible. And once he has finished describing hell, he places the pope right there. Next thing you know, we have a description of hell. There it is—in black and white. We know what hell is like. And Dante was just trying to take his revenge.

And then there are artists. They have never seen hell. But they read Dante's description, and they paint it. This is why we have this perennial problem. On one

111

hand, we have a very detailed explanation and detailed paintings of hell. The teeth, the nails, the eyes, the temperature. It's so cold that Satan is blue, yet there are fires everywhere.

On the other hand, we have only very general paintings of heaven. It has a gate, blue sky, some clouds, a little light, a little winged angel. That's all. Very plain, boring, contemporary type of décor.

Reasoning says, if there is a God, he must be like us—very judgmental. Everything is divided into good and bad. Very little ambiguity. "If you do this, this, and this, you're going to hell." Every religion has a hell and a heaven and a list of which actions will get you to hell and which will get you to heaven. If you are heading toward hell, there's a list of things you can do so you end up in heaven. Very convenient.

I'm not going to say, "What if heaven is here?" I *know* it is here. I am not going to say, "What if hell is here?" I *know* hell is here. Compared to some of the pain and suffering that human beings endure in their minds, it seems that boiling in oil would be just a bath in tepid water.

And heaven? The feeling of joy, the feeling of contentment, the feeling of peace. The feeling of being in love. When a human being is in love, there is a fullness inside. Is the described heaven, the reasoned heaven, any match for that? No. When a human being is content because they have felt peace within them, it surpasses all reasoned descriptions of heaven. In heaven, the temperature is supposed to be perfect. But when a person is content, it doesn't matter whether it is freezing cold or burning hot. Being content is being content. That's pure, pure heaven. That's when *true* divinity dances on a person's face, and it's unmistakable.

Divinity dances? Yes, it does. And clarity. And simplicity. All of these come to you one after another. It's never just one. They all come. For you. The possibilities are endless. All questions are resolved. This is what happens when clarity comes. You're left with understanding. Answers become apparent. Fulfillment comes, too. Here comes peace. Here is tranquility. Here is serenity. Here is joy. Just one after another.

When the heart finally feels full, you become content. And the moment becomes endless. Each breath becomes precious. All is put together. The fog is gone, and you begin to see.

It is so beautiful, that it is perfect. All that was dark, all that was hidden, is illuminated. And, because you can see, there is no fear. Do you know what it is like to be without fear? Do you?

When something is not illuminated, and you don't know what it is, there is fear.

Maybe you are the boss of six hundred people. You are in charge, and you have no fear. Really? Yes, you do. As soon as you cross the threshold of your home, fear comes. In the office, everybody follows your rules. Now, at home, you have to follow their rules. Everybody in your office was hoping you would not reject them. Now, you're home, and you're hoping your family will not reject you. The result: fear.

You don't have to be in fear. You can have the feeling of a true heaven within you. You don't have to reason it and believe in it. You can *know* it.

When the heart finally feels full, you become content.

The moment becomes endless. Each breath becomes precious. All is put together.

The fog is gone, and you begin to see.

It is so beautiful, that it is perfect. All that was hidden, is illuminated.

And, because you can see, there is no fear.

I THINK I HAD
A SANDWICH

It is amazing how we take all that is good in our lives and save it for last. Who came up with this idea? Maybe it started with desserts. I can understand that. Maybe some food tastes so pathetic that a "sugar hit" at the end is what you really need.

But life is not like that. Life is a beautiful journey that takes place every single day. It is dancing. It is calling you. It wants you to participate in it— to actively accept every gift that is placed before you every single day. Every moment. Without the judgment of good and bad. Without the judgment of right and wrong.

Recently, I was driving with someone who kept getting lost, even though the car had a navigation system. The next day, he said, "Oh, yesterday was a disaster!" No, it wasn't. Why wasn't it a disaster? Because he was alive. How easy it is to judge all the things that happen in our lives and throw away the value of breath, throw away the value of existence.

THE DIFFERENCE

Not too long ago, I went to a funeral. I had known that the time was coming close for this person, so before I left on a very long trip, I went to see him. I wanted to say goodbye while he was alive, because I really don't think you can say goodbye after someone's gone.

So I went to the funeral, and in a way, it was shocking. It wasn't this person leaving that was shocking, because that's what's going to happen to everyone. But at the cemetery, it was very obvious what all the headstones were saying: "Here lies a person."

At the cemetery, it was very obvious what all the headstones were saying: "Here lies a person."

I had to stop and reflect. This isn't just a headstone. This is a history. This was a person who was once alive. Good things happened and bad things happened. There were rough days and smooth days, confusing days and clear days. There were days that went this person's way and days that seemed to oppose him. A journey was made.

What is the difference between this headstone and me? One day, I, too, will be reduced to a headstone, with a name, a couple of dates, and a few messages chiseled out—and that's it. But am I not more than that?

There's no one like you. And there will be no one like you after you're gone.

Isn't life more than that? Doesn't existence itself rise above all the things that happen—the goods, the bads, the rights, the wrongs, the judgments? Isn't it a kindness to be here? Isn't this a special moment—this moment called being alive? How aware am I of it? How much do I recognize it?

What am I concerned about today? Am I the least bit concerned about something that is finer than the finest hair—something that cannot be measured in width, height, or weight and that is the only difference between me and that headstone? Do you know what it is? It's the breath that comes in and out of me.

You cannot take a picture of it. You cannot paint it. You cannot make a statue of it. You cannot give it, buy it, trade it, or sell it. And it makes all the difference between you and your headstone. Because breath comes, you're intelligent. Because it comes, you are Mr. So-and-So, Mrs. So-and-So, Miss So-and-So, Dr. So-and-So, Captain So-and-So, Professor So-and-So. And thanks to this gift of breath, you have the capability to understand, to question, to reason, to observe, and to learn.

IDEAS OF PEACE

Am I saving the possibility of being in peace for last? If I am, time out. A change of plans is required. That is not what I want to put off till the end. I need to feel peace every day that I am alive.

I go around the world talking about peace, and I have understood one thing: People don't even know what it is. Nobody has a clue.

Some people think that peace is when people put flowers in their hair and dance in the streets, and when they meet, they hug each other. When they go to a restaurant, if the waiter was good to them, then after they're finished, they pay the bill and give the waiter a hug—no more tips. That is their concept of peace.

Other people think peace is when all the fighting has stopped. Nobody will fight with anybody else. If your neighbor does something annoying, you'll just sit there and pout. And some people think that peace will be the day the trains stop running and dogs stop barking.

Some people think peace is being on top of a mountain overlooking a beautiful lake at sunset. When you hear crickets, you say, "Oh, it's so peaceful." Next time you see a cricket, don't just shoo it away—it's associated with peace. Of course, if that same cricket ends up in your bedroom, then peace is over; you declare war on it. And it is not a question of "wanted: dead or alive." You want it dead!

REAL PEACE

The peace I am talking about is the peace without which we would lose the very fabric of who we are, the peace that dances in the heart of everyone. The reality. The beauty. The joy. The true peace—not an absence of something, but the very presence of something. That is what is alive. That is what is possible. Even in the middle of a war, a person can experience this peace.

Some people think freedom is when you get away from your house for the weekend. To teenagers, freedom is when they leave their parents' house. Freedom to parents is when their teenagers actually leave, not just threaten to leave, but actually leave. Is that freedom?

Freedom from my troubles. Is that freedom? Freedom from my concerns. Is that freedom? Freedom from my responsibilities. Is that freedom?

I talk about a freedom that can be felt even in a prison. That's the freedom that no one can take away from me. Peace that cannot be disturbed—that is real peace. Freedom that cannot be taken away—that is real freedom.

118

TWO WAYS

We create and define our systems. People are still trying to define what God is. One of the definitions is, "God is indefinable." So we say, "Let's define that." One person says, "Be free of those ideas and concepts." And the other one says, "No, I love my concepts. There's nothing wrong with them." It becomes very personal. People get so caught up in definitions, ideas, and concepts. And then the world engages in a fight: "There's only one God. But my God is better than your God." Do you find that logical?

We have two ways of taking in information. One is theoretical; the other is practical. And between the theory and the practical lies a big mountain called *understanding*. On one side of the mountain is theory—keep talking, keep defining. On the other side of the mountain lies this wonderful phenomenon of feeling. So what is the difference between the two?

Let's say you went into a restaurant, sat down, and ordered a sandwich. You waited and waited, and then the waiter brought you the bill. You said, "But where's my sandwich?" And he said, "I brought you the sandwich; you ate it." There are actually people who would pay the bill and walk away totally confused.

All day long they would keep thinking, "Did I eat the sandwich? I'm still hungry. Maybe it was a little sandwich. Did I really eat it?" They would go home, sit down with their wife, and say, "Honey, is it possible to eat a sandwich and not know it?" Then they would go to the library. "I think I had a sandwich, but I really didn't have a sandwich—do you have a book on that?" "No." "Okay. I'll go look at the self-help section." That'd be a great book: *You Thought You Had a Sandwich, but Did You?* It would be a big seller. People could relate to it.

You are the only one who can decide whether or not you are feeling peace. It is not dependent on somebody saying, "By the way, you're experiencing peace. So keep quiet." No. *You* have the last word. You have to feel that peace, that freedom, not just write "I feel free" three hundred times.

A MIRROR

Some people say, "I heard his speech; it was nice, but he didn't give us anything concrete." What can I give you when you already have all that you need within you? It's like, what could you possibly give to a beautiful woman? If she's really beautiful, you could give her a mirror and tell her, "See what I see every day." I think that would be a romantic compliment.

Maybe it is possible that the woman would take it the wrong way and ask you, "Why are you giving me a mirror? What's wrong with me?" It's funny, but that's

119

why we look at ourselves in the mirror—to see the faults. "Is my tie crooked? Is something stuck in my teeth?"

People stand in front of the *Mona Lisa*, and they all gawk and say, "Beautiful." There should be a mirror! Because there is no one like you on the face of this earth. Not even if you have a twin. There's no one like you. And there will be no one like you after you're gone.

This is your time to begin to understand. And here is the concrete thing: to start to realize that all you ever wanted, you have. You have that freedom and that peace inside of you.

This is what I offer people—a mirror. What else can you give to someone who has everything? You have everything! That which is within you is, by its very nature, divine. By its very existence, it is the most beautiful symphony. By its very existence, it is the most beautiful play ever written. You are the actor, and the most incredible script has been written for you. There is love. There's a little bit of action. There's a little bit of clarity and a little bit of confusion. It's an amazing script. How well are you playing it? How well do you know your lines? How well do you know this play? Do you need somebody in the orchestra pit to read you the script?

When you don't know, you need somebody to whisper your lines. How many of you know about the people who are whispering your lines in your life? And when two of them start speaking at the same time, what happens? Family feud? "I want you to be this way," "I want you to be that way," "I want you to do this for me," "I want you to do that for me," "I trusted you." No. You expected. Don't bring trust into it. You don't even know what trust is.

Peace that cannot be disturbed —that is real peace.

Freedom that cannot be taken away —that is real freedom.

120

Trust is meant to be for the coming and going of your breath—that it will come and it will go. Trust, not an expectation. Will tomorrow come? Are you expecting it to come? Or are you trusting it to come? Think about it. If it doesn't come, there's nothing you can do about it. You can't argue. You can't complain. Wise are the ones who begin to understand the value of what they have been given while it's still being given. Understanding the value of something when it is gone is too easy.

Begin to acknowledge your existence in the simplest way possible—by going within. Not from ideas, but from your understanding. Not measuring with the scales of what you do not have.

Understand what you *do* have. Because what you do have is right here within you, and it's everything. And when I say everything, I mean *everything*.

THE TIE BUSINESS
People say, "I'm a father." No, you're a human being. They say, "I'm a mother." No, you're a human being. But we don't see human beings; we see everything else. We think a person is important because he's wearing a tie. I know this tie business really well. The tie is an amazing tool. Put it on, and you're somebody; take it off, and people won't even hold an elevator door for you.

We have trained ourselves to see the differences—our color, our height. The taller you are, the more likely you are to be successful. At what? Banging your head? You will do a lot of that.

We look at all the differences. See the similarity. You were born. That you are alive is a blessing unparalleled. You exist. Understand that.

REMINDING
I'm talking about the presence of a beauty that is inside of you, through which you have everything and without which you have nothing.

You are so fortunate that you are alive. That is simple. That is real. I just wanted to remind you of that because in times of trouble, we forget the most important thing. And that's what gets us into trouble.

You know this. You know everything I have said. You know that peace is beautiful. Now the time has come to actually feel that peace in your life. Nobody is too young, and nobody is too old. Now is the time to understand. Understand. Then you won't need all the explanations. When understanding kicks in, that's all you need.

In life, know. In life, understand. Let every step be real. Not somebody's instruction from the orchestra pit: "Now say this." Because this is a matter of life. You have one life. One existence. One incredible gift that you have been given.

122

I love to learn. I love to understand. A long time ago, someone showed me how to look within, and I did. And I'm happy I did. I'm thankful I did. I'm thankful for every day. And I'm still learning the art of unlearning how to be distracted.

It is crucial to remember what is important. The more important something is, the more important it is to remember it. And you must also understand how likely you are to forget it. That's how we are.

It is my privilege to remind you. It is my privilege, my joy, my honor, to go around the world and tell people about the possibility of being in peace.

It is a message of the heart. I don't prepare my speeches. If you had asked me what I was going to talk about when I came here, I wouldn't have known. I come, I open my heart, and with a sense of clarity, a sense of understanding, and hopefully with humility, I present what I have to say. I have nothing to sell. Some people always think, "Oh, there must be some hidden motive." Do you live like that? Every time you're nice to somebody, is there some hidden motive?

Your life, your breath, your existence is good. It has been given to you. The motive is kindness.

Peace is not an abstract concept. Peace is a feeling. Peace is real. It isn't about a flower giving off a beautiful blue hue. It is about feeling a feeling inside and saying, "Yes!" because you have felt it. Not like that person who says, "I think I ate the sandwich," but like the one who says, "I *know* I ate the sandwich," and being happy because you enjoyed your sandwich. Not walking around wondering, "Did I really eat that sandwich? Where is that sandwich?"

There's no room for that in this life.

"Did I really eat that sandwich?"

123

We breed unconsciousness,
and then we wonder
what happens to us in our life.

Look again at those seeds
you have been given
and make some simple decisions.

124

THE SEEDS OF LIFE

This is a metaphor, but it's true: When we come into this world, we're given seeds, and the question is, what will we do with these seeds? And what are these seeds?

There is a seed of anger, but there is also a seed of kindness. There is a seed of love and a seed of understanding. And there is a seed of doubt and a seed of confusion. Whatever seed you have sown in your garden of life ultimately determines the tree you're going to sit under. How restful it will be depends on what kind of seed you have sown.

There are certain trees that have beautiful flowers, but they produce a sap that does not allow grass to grow beneath them. Every seed has a particular quality, something that it offers. When it is sown, and it grows and becomes a tree, it will have very particular characteristics that you may or may not like.

I'm not passing judgment or saying what kind of seed you should have sown. I merely point out some of the characteristics of different trees. You are capable of making that decision for yourself. You have enough intelligence to choose—from a place of clarity—what will benefit you the most. Human beings, as long as they can see clearly, will make the right decision.

THE TREE OF ANGER

It is not only a question of sowing the seeds, but also nurturing them, watering them, protecting them, taking care of them so that they grow.

Most of us have sown the seed of anger. There seems to be no hesitation to go near it, but we don't like the droppings from this tree. And you promise yourself you will never go near this tree again. But either you forget or you have become so used to living unconsciously, that there is no hesitation to go right back to that tree and get its sap all over you again. It's disgusting, and sometimes this sap is so nasty that it can take a lifetime to get rid of it. Two people love each other, and then each one in turn visits their own little Anger Tree, and then it's, "I hate you. I wish you were never born."

So, that is a good example of a seed and a tree. If you planted a seed and nurtured it, there will be a tree. If you want to know what you have been nurturing, just open the window and look in your garden, and see the trees that are there.

THE TREE OF DOUBT

People plant the seed of doubt: "Is it really going to happen?" The tree of doubt comes. It is also disgusting, because dust comes off of it that gets all over the place, and it takes what could be beautiful and turns it into nothing.

In life, one of the biggest lessons you have to learn—and this is going to sound funny since we're talking about doubt—is that you have to give every single new day the benefit of the doubt. This is a positive doubt. Negative doubt is, "Oh, my God. Something is wrong." Positive doubt is, "You know what? I have been in this world for so many years. Maybe what this person is going to say to me today will be different."

But that is not the nature of the tree of doubt. It doubts everything. It doubts your ability to understand your experience, your life. All because a seed was sown—a seed of doubt.

126

ME AND MY SHADOW

If you look in your garden, you may not see a tree of understanding. So you might say, "Hmm. Which tree is that?" But that is because that seed never got sown. But the beautiful thing is, no matter when you sow these seeds, they will sprout. It's never too late.

But what is the tree of understanding? We are taught to believe, to "take a leap of faith." But you don't *have* to do that. It could be very risky. Instead of just believing, you can actually understand what it means to be alive.

You might think, "I know what it means to be alive." No, you don't. You associate your life with your job, with the things that happen around you. That is not your life.

There is a big difference between your shadow and you, is there not? Yes, you have a shadow, but you are not your shadow. This is the distinction you have to remember. Some things exist because you exist, but they are not your existence. They may appear and disappear, but you will still be.

How unfortunate it is that we start associating ourselves with those things until we think, "They are me; I am them." No. They are there, but you aren't them. We have a huge stew cooking, and everything is in it. After it has cooked long enough, we won't be able to tell the carrots from the peas or the potatoes from the onions.

The hub is your existence: your life, your understanding, your steps, your journey, your elation and the process of filling your heart with utter and total contentment.

SATISFIED OR CONTENT?

Do you want to be satisfied? Or content? Which one? You can learn to be satisfied, but contentment comes naturally.

Most of us have sown the seed of anger. But we don't like the droppings from this tree.

If you want to know what you have been nurturing —just open the window, look in your garden, and see the trees that are there.

Contentment is a feeling that emanates from within you—from your basic core. It is not the same as being able to say, "I don't need anything anymore." That is being satisfied. And many people confuse being satisfied with being content. They say, "People who are content don't want anything else; therefore, they have given up the world, their children, their houses, their jobs. They've given up everything. They live on some mountain and have become holy." Have you ever seen a "holy" man in his "holy" wardrobe? Every day, he wears special clothes to let people know he has renounced the world. Is he not thinking of the world when he puts his clothes on? Of course he is. He needs to announce that he has renounced.

Somebody asks you, "Are you satisfied?" You can say, "Yes. I have a good job. I have a good family. I have a good car. I have great friends. And even my pets listen to me. So I must be satisfied." Ah. But are you content? "Mmm, I don't know, but I'm satisfied." But are you content? Did you sow the seed of contentment?

THE SEED OF LOVE
Did you sow the seed of love? I'm not talking about lust. I *know* you have sown that. Those are the first ones that get sown. Anger begins early. Frustration, early. Lust? Early—or semi-early.

Love is different. What is the difference between a butterfly and a kite? Both fly. A kite is tethered to the kite string. Without that string, it will falter and fall. A butterfly, on the other hand, is not tethered to a string, and it flies. And, if you were to tie it to a kite string, it would falter and fall. Love is like a butterfly. Lust is like a kite. Big difference between the two.

128

Love dances in the heart of the one who loves. Love not only makes the one who feels it feel good, but all those who are around also begin to feel it. There's a saying: "The world loves a lover." Because that is how love is.

Have you sown the seed of joy? What are the seeds of joy? Does joy have anything to do with bank accounts? No. A bank account equals convenience. It's convenient to have enough money, that's all. Were the Roman emperors really happy? Never. There was a stretch of time when one emperor after another was assassinated. I mean, they knew what was going to happen to them. They always had to watch their backs and try their hardest to get rid of anybody they thought was their enemy before the person could kill them.

SEEDS OF UNCONSCIOUSNESS

And then, people look for reasons for everything. And karma becomes really popular with people who are suffering. "Why is this happening to me? Must be my karma, something I did in a past lifetime." It wouldn't have anything to do with what you have chosen to do in this life, would it? All the unconsciousness that you bred?

If your job is to milk venom from a king cobra, don't be too surprised if one day the cobra bites you. That is its nature. Maybe the cobra is agitated that day. Maybe he knows what you're going to do, and he doesn't really want to donate his venom. Maybe the last time you did it, you squeezed his head a little too hard, and he's mad at you. Maybe he thinks you're bringing food. Who knows?

But we breed unconsciousness, and then we wonder what happens to us in our life. It cannot be. Look again at those seeds you have been given and make some simple decisions. Especially if you look in your heart and find that a few trees are missing that you think should've been there, that you assumed were there. No problem. It's never too late. Seeds are in hand; sow them. Take care of them.

FOR WHOM?

Nurture kindness in your life, and you will be rewarded with the gift of kindness. Sow the seed of love, and you will be rewarded with that most incredible feeling of love dancing in your heart. Sow the seed of understanding, and you will be rewarded with understanding. Sow the seed of clarity, and you will be rewarded with clarity.

Then in this life, every day, a tribute of gratitude can be paid. Right now, you don't have time. You are too busy cleaning the sap from the Anger Tree, the Misunderstanding Tree, the Hate Tree.

However it is, do not sow seeds of unconsciousness anymore. Really nasty stuff. Stinks. Sow consciousness, and the reward will be a simple and beautiful reality.

Enjoy this life, because that's one thing you can do with it. And it's good. It's all very good. But not through the eyes of doubt, not through the eyes of anger, not through the eyes of hate. I'm not saying you should love everyone and walk around saying, "I love you, I love you, I love you." That's not what I am talking about.

The tree of love is not planted in your neighbor's garden. Don't even try going to your neighbor's garden to plant that tree. The tree of love is planted in your garden. And why should you plant it? Maybe you think you should become kind so that other people will be kind to you. That's not the reason why you should be kind.

To feel kindness. To feel true love. To understand what it is like not to be in doubt. To understand that there is a place where there are answers—this is something you do for you, not for other people.

Then, of course, some people say, "Isn't that selfish?" Is it? When I understand something, am I robbing somebody else of that understanding? Is there only a limited number of understandings, so that if I get one, somebody else won't get it? If that is how it is, then it is selfish, and you shouldn't understand something, because somebody else might need that understanding more than you do.

But that is not how it is. When you understand something, you're not depriving anybody of that understanding. When you receive an answer, you do not deprive anybody of that answer. The other person can receive it, too. That is what is so beautiful. It is not at somebody else's expense; it is just about you. Your journey, your existence. Your heart, your contentment. Your life. And you are not depriving anybody of anything by taking as much as you can.

Do whatever you have to do in your life. But do this, too: sow the seeds that you want to sow. Nurture them. Garner them. Help them grow. And then you will be able to enjoy the trees in your garden of life.

130

WHAT IS GOOD FOR YOU?

We tend to analyze everything. But when I feel thirsty, I don't want an analysis of water. I don't want descriptions of water. All I want to know is how to get water so I can quench my thirst. That's the point—to quench the thirst.

Whatever we do—whether it is exploring space, mapping the bottom of the ocean, flying a kite, bungee jumping, learning how to cook, designing new airplanes, inventing new technologies—we do because we think it will benefit us. And we have a bad habit of jumping into things without ever looking back and asking, "Did this really benefit me?" We just go on with new invention after new invention.

I look at pictures of myself when I was a baby and wonder, "Where did he go? Did he die?" It's a weird question, because I know that baby was me and that I am alive. But I don't look anything like that baby. So, looking from there to here, I can't help but ask, "Where did he go?"

We think we are the sum of all the things we do, and yet that picture of me as a baby was just one snapshot in a life—my life—which now I understand is never constant. A picture of me three years from now will look different. Ten years from now, it will look even more different, and twenty years from now, it will look very, very different. I am constantly changing. I may not perceive the change as it happens, but I am changing.

So who am I? Who are you? We have a singular quest to better ourselves—to evolve, to move forward, to improve upon all that can be improved. To make it better.

My message is about the possibility of the ultimate betterment of a human being—not of mankind, not of a country, not of a social belief, but of a human being. And it is not through religion or doctrine, not through ideas or concepts. Neither is it through hearsay or repetition or through the sheep effect. It is through each individual exploring and finding the beauty within themselves. And all that is asked of a person is to clean their plate.

TWO ANTS
Once, two ants met. One ant lived on a hill that was made out of sugar. The other ant lived on a hill made out of salt.

"Where are you from?" asked the salt ant.

"I live on the sugar hill."

"Sugar hill? What is sugar?"

"Oh, it's this wonderful, sweet-tasting stuff."

And the salt ant said, "I've never heard of that. I'm from the salt hill. I eat salt, and it makes me thirsty. But this sweet stuff sounds pretty good!"

So the ant from the sugar hill said, "Why don't you come over one day, and you can taste it and see if you like it?"

132

So the ant decided, "Yeah, a new taste. That's a good idea."

They agreed on a date. The day came, and soon the salt ant was getting ready to go. "Hmm," he thought, "I'm going all the way to this sugar hill. What if I don't like it? What if it tastes terrible? Then I'll be hungry. I know what I'm going to do. I'm going to bring some salt with me, so I'll have it in case I don't like sugar." He put some salt in his mouth and took off.

When the salt ant arrived, the sugar ant was glad to see him. "Hey, how are you doing?"

"Oh, I'm good. I just can't wait to taste the sugar! It sounds great."

"Here. Taste it."

The salt ant put the sugar in his mouth, chewed on it a little bit, and said, "It tastes just like salt."

"Really?"

"Yeah! It tastes just like my salt—there's no difference. I guess you call it 'sugar' here, and we call it 'salt' where I live. It's the same thing!"

The sugar ant said, "I don't think so. Open your mouth. Let me take a look."

Sure enough, in the back of his mouth, there was some salt. So the sugar ant said, "Let me have that," and he took it out. "Now, taste the sugar."

"Wow! Unbelievable. It's so different, so amazing! I *love* this stuff! I'm moving!"

This would not have been the outcome had the salt remained in the ant's mouth. That's why I say, "Clean the plate and taste the dish as it should be tasted—not mixed with anything else. Taste it so you will know what its flavor is."

I am talking about something that is not a blend. It is not about your accomplishments. It is about *you*—you being alive. I know one thing, and it is almost ridiculously simple: The coming and the going of the breath is the most amazing thing happening in your life.

"What?" you might ask. "It isn't my new job? My new wife? My new husband? My new girlfriend? My new dog? It isn't my new hairdo, my new nails, my new dress, my new house?" No.

You might think, "But there are a lot of wonderful things in this world." Yes, I agree. There's a lot of beautiful scenery—beautiful mountains, clouds, lakes, oceans, beaches, and palm trees. There are beautiful fruits, flowers, birds, animals. But you can only see, feel, touch, smell any of those because breath is coming in and out of you. Without the breath being present, someone could place as many flowers as they wanted under your nose, and they would get no response whatsoever.

WHAT IS GOOD FOR YOU?

If you have a bad memory, the problem is you don't know what you forgot. In certain circumstances, this can be blissful, but it's mostly the other way around. All that is truly good for you, you forget. All that is truly bad for you, you remember like it only happened two seconds ago.

Do you know what is good for you? Before you answer this question, I want to remind you that when you were very young, you knew what was good for you. You didn't think of it that way. You just went about doing it. What was it? You wanted to be happy. You really didn't care about anything else. You just wanted to be happy. That's all. It was a simple time.

It didn't matter if you were born into a poor family or a rich family. You just wanted to be happy. Then slowly, slowly, a lot happened. Step by step your attention was diverted from happiness to becoming a slave of the world. You were being tempered so that the world would be able to withstand you and you would be able to withstand the world. Responsibilities, discipline, and all that. Do this, do this, do that, do that. But you were not being disciplined into what was your innate feeling from the beginning before anybody got hold of your brain.

I see this happening everywhere, and it irks me, but I can't do anything about it. A lot of people think things are not so bad. I'm not here to judge, but in my opinion, if ever a report card was given out on this world, it would have an F on it.

THE ANIMAL KINGDOM

I was watching a TV show where they depicted all the things that happen when they film the show. One guy was trying to get friendly with an elephant, and the elephant just picked him up with his trunk and shook him. Now, I'd like to see that guy pick up the elephant and shake *him*. There would be no contest. Porpoises can swim faster than we can. Sharks have evolved a perfect set of teeth. They don't ever have to see a dentist. If a tooth falls out, it's not a problem—a new one will grow. And sharks don't even need teeth—they can gum you to death.

We needed to invent an airplane to fly, but birds and insects didn't have to invent anything to fly. And we're so proud because we invented the GPS. Our sense of direction is pathetic. A pigeon that has a brain no bigger than our earlobe doesn't need a GPS. It has one built in. In the old days, people actually used pigeons to carry messages. Wherever they went, when the pigeons were released, they knew how to get back home.

134

The whales must look at us and say, "I can talk halfway around the world, and it's free. I don't need cell towers; the signal is always there."

Communication? We have invented cell phones. The whales must look at us and say, "I can talk halfway around the world, and it's free. I don't need cell towers; the signal is always there."

With so many of what we think of as *our* inventions, we are just barely reaching the minimal mark of the animal kingdom. And yet, most of those creatures feel free to do what they have to do. With all our inventions, we are so trapped that we have forgotten our basic fundamental desire to be content.

NO INTERPRETATIONS

In your life, you need peace. You need to be content. You need to be happy. You need to feel like the child that you once were, that you still are! No matter how many turns you have taken in your life or how many changes have happened, these fundamentals have not changed. So, if you need to discover something, discover your thirst to be happy and content.

Discover the joy that resides in the heart of every human being. Be fulfilled. Not by questions but by answers. For some people, this sounds strange. "What? No questions? Just answers? Aren't questions and answers always paired?" No. They are not. That's why people never find the answers. They just keep finding more questions.

When I first came to Boulder, Colorado, back in the '70s, people would come every day to ask me questions. There was an Indian man who had studied the *Bhagavad Gita.* And every time he had a chance, he'd ask questions about the Gita: "Why did this person say that? What does this mean? What does that mean?" Again and again. So finally, I said to him, "In the Gita, Arjuna has questions, and Krishna is answering them.

136

And as the Gita progresses, Arjuna has fewer and fewer questions. Finally, it gets to the point that Arjuna has no more questions."

So I said, "Don't you ever wonder what happened to make him stop asking questions? That's what you need to find out."

Do you know how much interpretation goes on in the world? I watch the news, and they give me interpretations. They should just show me what happened and let me figure it out myself. But they say, "This is what was said. Let me give you my interpretation. This is what was meant." And I say, "Do I look deficient to you? Like I can't make up my own mind? Like I don't have a brain? Like I can't think?"

The whole point of what I talk about is for you to be able to drink the water yourself—not for somebody else to drink the water and tell you how good it was. You are the one who is thirsty, and you need to drink the water yourself. No explanations, no interpretations.

YOUR OWN IDEA
There are a lot of ideas piled on our shoulders that are not ours. They were placed there by other people. We love to pass on our ideas to others: "This is what it is; this is how it is." Let go of these ideas. They are not yours. What is your own idea? It is the same one you've always had—to be happy. That's *your* idea. And you don't have to let go of that.

Maybe you have figured this out, but certain things make you feel really good. And if you made a list of all those things, guess what would be on the top? Peace. Peace makes you feel the best. Watching a good movie? That can make you feel okay. Comedy can make you feel good. Some people like massage. That makes them feel good. Some people like to eat ice cream.

But of all the things that we do in our lives to feel good, peace makes us feel the best. Contentment makes us feel the best. There are many things in this world that have strings attached. Contentment doesn't. Peace doesn't.

Sometimes people fall in love, and they go around saying, "I'm in love; I'm in love." Two months later, they say, "I hate that person." It can all just reverse itself.

Peace is not like that. Peace is always good. Where is it? It's already within you.

**You are the one
who is thirsty,
and you need to drink
the water yourself.**

**No explanations,
No interpretations.**

DON'T EXPLAIN IT – FEEL IT

What we sometimes forget, and it's not a question of sometimes, but most of the time, is what is variable and what is permanent.

We are on this boat that's going down the river, and somehow we have convinced ourselves—how, I don't know—that the boat is not moving. Every time we look up, we see the scenery changing, and we say to ourselves, "Amazing. The earth is moving! Look at all those trees—they are moving. Look at all those houses—they are moving. Because, surely, the boat that I am in is not moving."

We are trying to conquer the "Grand Illusion." But it'll go on. All the things that we are trying to stop or get on top of will be there long after we've gone. The only thing that won't be here is you. You are the variable. It's not the trees or the houses that are moving. You are moving. You may not like it, but that's the truth.

When we don't like to face the truth, we try to explain it away. We want to explain life, explain what is good, explain what is truth. And these are things that can only be felt but not explained. If you are thirsty, you cannot satisfy the thirst by explaining water. You need to drink it. If you are hungry, you cannot satisfy your hunger by explaining food. You need to eat it.

You cannot explain what life means. You need to feel it. You cannot explain your breath. You need to breathe it. You cannot explain what this existence means. It can only be felt. If you understand that, an entirely different door opens up to you. You begin to understand by feeling—not through explanations. You begin to understand the preciousness of life, the joy, and the truest responsibility to be in gratitude to the most magnificent power that has made it possible for you to be alive.

Not just for one minute, five minutes, ten minutes. To actually feel the eternal gratitude. That's what it means to be alive. Not doubt. Not confusion. That's not being alive. Not pain, not suffering, not misery, not darkness. Not sorrow and lamenting and wishing. Being alive means to be crystal clear.

WISHING, WISHING
You have been wishing since you were very young. And at the end of each wish, did you not tell yourself that if this wish came true, this would be it, no more wishes? And when the wish came true, did you stop wishing? No. You had a new wish.

In your life, it has not been that your wishes haven't come true. Actually, if you look back, more wishes have come true than you even care to remember. But you were never careful about what you wished. Just wish, wish, wish. And *boom!* They came true.

It's amazing how many wishes have come true. But what did you wish for? Did you wish for contentment? No. You used your wishes to try to be content the way you thought would bring contentment. First, you were on your feet, going everywhere. Walking, walking, walking. And you were healthy. Then what did you wish for? "I wish I had a bicycle so I could get around quicker." So you got a bicycle, but you still had a problem. Somebody might steal the bicycle, so you had to buy a lock and key.

When it's raining and you're walking, you can find a dry place somewhere to stand. If you have a bicycle, you have to figure out what to do with it.

So, once you realized the bicycle was no good, what did you wish for? You did not wish to have the bicycle taken away. You wished for a scooter. *Then* everything would be fine. Now, of course, once you have a scooter and then a helmet, you fall down and break your elbow. More problems. But did you wish for the scooter to be taken away? No. Now you want a car. And by the time you get your car, you forget why you even needed a car. But now you have one.

IMAGINING THE PERFECT

And the car brings more problems. You have to get your driver's license and insurance, make car payments, keep the car clean. But when you were wishing for your car, the car you imagined never needed gasoline, never needed maintenance, never needed spare tires, never had any problems. It was the perfect car that just ran and ran and went much faster than even possible. And it was always the perfect temperature inside the car because it was all in the imagination.

Imagination. What have you imagined for yourself? Unfortunately, you've even imagined how God should be, with a little help from those who whisper in your ear, "God is like this and God is like that." You have imagined God. And not only have you imagined God, but you have also imagined how your whole life is going to be, haven't you?

In your imagination, you have a perfect picture—just like you had of the car that never needs gasoline, is always at the perfect temperature, never breaks down, never needs washing or waxing or a parking space.

You have imagined this entire existence and what it means. Day after day, this monster that you have created could never survive except that you keep feeding it with explanations. Every day, you have to explain what happened. You have to explain what it means to be alive. You have excuses for why you were unable to feel gratitude, why you lived another day unconsciously, why you stayed away from all that you know, in your heart of hearts, is good. Another day and another day and another day. And before you know it, you run out of days.

And then you know! You know all that you should have done. You finally know without a doubt all that you *should* have done. But now you don't have the means to do it!

WILL YOU COME BACK?

Shocking, isn't it? People have explanations for that, too: "Life is cruel." Or, "It's okay. I'll be back." How do you know?

It is very important to have memory. If you have an iPod, first you need to know if it is yours or not. Somebody else's isn't going to have your music on it. It's very important to remember. Otherwise, you wouldn't know if this was your house, or car, or watch, or jacket, or shoes. When you go from this world, all that is severed.

Why are there so many explanations of how to get to heaven? "This is how you get to salvation; this is how you get to heaven. Just do this, this, this. No problem." When people tell me this, I always say, "Are you coming with me to guarantee it?" What if at the gates of heaven, they said, "Nope." Then I'll call that person over and say, "Talk to this guy. He said no." And, of course, I would tell the person, "I have two pieces of bad news: one, I'm not getting in; and, two, you're not getting in, either."

Gates of heaven. Why gates? We picture God with big eyes. Why eyes? *You* need eyes, not God. If a car created you, you wouldn't have eyes; you would have headlights. You wouldn't have eyelids; you would have wipers. You wouldn't have teeth; you would have a radiator. And you wouldn't have hands; you would have wheels. If a car created you, that's what it would do. And when human beings try to create a god, that's exactly what they do. Eyes, judgmental; heaven, gates. The creator of all those things is not God; this is man's imagination. This is human beings: have a gate and a gatekeeper!

Don't you think God could have come up with a better system than to have a gatekeeper and a book? Of course. But this is a car creating a human. This is a human creating heaven.

It is your boat that is moving, not the trees, not the houses.

They will be here after you have gone. And others will pass and make the same mistake as you did.

HOME IS NOW

People have their explanations, their ideas, but heaven is here—now! It's not about your future and not about your past but about this moment. This moment is singular in nature. Beautiful, pleasant. Peaceful. Enjoyable by all human beings. It is so beautiful, so amazing that even *hearing* about it can bring peace in a person's life. That is its nature.

It is in this single moment that you exist. Feel at home in this moment. You have made yourself feel at home in tomorrow. That's not yours. Feel at home in this moment called *now*. Feel at home in gratitude. Feel at home in peace, not in confusion. Feel at home in the feeling, not in explanations. Feel at home in your truest self.

If you want to be independent, then be independent of confusion. Be independent of doubt. Be independent of all that is not yours. And feel. Feel reality in its magnificence. Not from fear. Because fear is not yours, either. You were made to behold joy.

This is what belongs in this vessel, in this human body. This is what it was made for. Not all the other stuff.

So, what are you going to do? I know there are people who are going to talk about it, try to explain the unexplainable. Don't waste your time.

YOUR CHOICE
Who you listen to is up to you. That's always your choice. You can listen to the voice inside of you that says, "Everything is wrong." Or you can listen to the voice that says, "Be. Be free. Be clear. Enjoy this life. Enjoy this existence."

Many people will tell you that you don't have a choice. I tell you, I *know* you have a choice. Every day you hear the two voices; you have a choice which one to listen to. You won't be able to stop hearing them. That is the nature of ears. But which one you pay attention to is up to you. It's not up to the voice. Knowing—that's half the battle. Know. Understand. And be fulfilled. Every day. No excuses. No explanations. Be fulfilled every single day.

I'm on my way to India to little villages that I didn't even know existed there. Talk about explanations. There are so many explanations in India. When I talk, people say, "I have never heard that explanation before!"

When I tell them, "This is not an explanation. I'm offering you the real thing," they are shocked. "Really? This is not your imagination?" "No. This is real." You can feel it. You can feel that peace in your life. This is not just pictures of wells and rivers and people dancing in the water. This is the real thing. It's so straightforward. It's so simple.

So, take the steps in this life. Know it is your boat that is moving, not the trees, not the houses. They will be here after you have gone, and others will pass and make the same mistake as you did. But you can know who is moving and who is not. You don't need to make mistakes. Enjoy.

It is in this single moment that you exist.

Feel at home in this moment.

You have made yourself
feel at home in tomorrow.
That's not yours.

Feel at home in this
moment called now.

Feel at home in gratitude.

Feel at home in peace,
not in confusion.

Feel at home in the feeling,
not in explanations.

Feel at home in
your truest self.

Look in your heart, and you will find
the true essence of your existence.

Look within, and you will find
the most beautiful waters.

Look within, and you will find
answers to which you don't even have questions.

PART FOUR

YOUR HOME
OF EXISTENCE

The important question is, what do I choose every day?

LIVING IN AN EVER-CHANGING WORLD

Everything is transient. That is its nature. The universe is never still. It is constantly moving. Nothing in the universe—even the universe itself—lasts forever. Once it was not, and once again it won't be. At one time, you, too, were not. And once again, you will not be. Your life is not about when you were not. And it is not about when you will no longer be. It is about when you *are*.

You shouldn't be obsessed with what could happen after you die. You should be obsessed with what is happening—that you are alive now, because that is where the celebration is. What I talk about is not comtemplation, but experience. It is not about a theory; it is about reality. Do you know that reality does not exist in the past? And do you know that reality does not exist in the future? There is only one place reality can be, and that is now.

If there is a truth, that truth is *now*. And there is no greater truth that can be spoken than to say, "I am alive."

WHAT DO I CHOOSE?
I came into this world—I don't remember it. Most people don't seem to. There is a picture of me when I was little that I can remember being taken. And from then on, I remember things. A lot has happened in my life. Many stories, many war wounds. And I know that everything in my life has changed.

Everything that I thought would never change has changed. Everything I didn't want to change has also changed. And, conveniently, everything I did want to change also has changed. There have been only two constants in my life. One is change. And the other is the desire to be fulfilled. To be content. To be happy. To feel a heart full of gratitude again and again.

You can acquire a lot of objects in this world, and you will grow tired of them, believe me. But you will never, ever grow tired of a heart welling up with gratitude—no matter how many times it has happened before. Every time your heart fills with gratitude, it feels like it is the first time. New? Yes. Exceptional? Yes. Gratifying? There is no greater gratification.

The desire for that feeling has been a constant in my life. So has everything changing on the outside. Every day I have to make a lot of decisions. Sometimes they come fast and furiously. Some days, I'm just inundated with questions wherever I turn— question, question, question. Right down to the point of what I want to eat.

But those are not the important questions. The important question is, what do I choose every day? I have to invest. Time is pouring down. There is nothing I can do about it. Nothing. I can't slow it down; I can't speed it up. It just keeps coming, coming, coming.

What do I do with my time? Do I save it? Do I conquer it? Do I capture it? Or do I just let it go? Came/went, came/went, came/went. And keep being surprised. "Huh? Huh? Huh?" That's what can happen.

I remember when I was young, older people always used to tell me, "The older you get, the quicker time will go." I understand that now. But I also understand that

150

There is no greater truth that can be spoken than to say, "I am alive."

it doesn't go any quicker or any slower. It's flowing at the same rate—it's only my perspective that has changed.

THE MUTE EATING CANDY
The human being seeks immortality in a mortal world. Excuse me. You shouldn't be seeking immortality. You won't find it.

Seek the immortal; it resides in you. It always has, always will. And then you can make time work for you instead of you working for it.

Do you know that you have integrity? Not because of your accomplishments—but just as a human being who walks this earth, who has been given the chance to be, to feel, to understand. And in this world, you are robbed of your integrity. You are robbed of your understanding of who you are.

How do you avoid being robbed? How do you save your integrity? The fifteenth-century Indian poet Kabir says that nobody—*nobody*—is poor. And Kabir was so poor that he even wrote that he had no idea where his next meal was going to come from.

What did he mean, then, that nobody is poor? "Nobody's poor—everybody's rich. But we have forgotten to open the package that was sent with us, and that is why we are penniless." This is what he said. What package? Did we come with a package? Yes. Where is it? It's right here—in this human existence.

This package of human life has riches beyond belief. Gratitude, fulfillment, understanding, joy. Do you really understand what the word *joy* means?

Joy comes whenever you feel the immortal inside of you. That's what fills you with joy. And what is joy like? Indescribable. What does contentment feel like? It cannot be described. What does peace feel like? Again, Kabir says, "It cannot be described. It is like a mute person eating candy."

151

Just because that person cannot describe the candy doesn't mean he cannot enjoy it. His enjoyment has nothing to do with his inability to describe it. Even if he wanted to describe it, and he wasn't mute, all he could say was, "Mmm. Mmm. Mmm."

There are two kinds of teachers. One says, "I will eat the candy, and then I'll tell you about it. I'll write about it." But when you ask a real teacher, "What does the candy taste like?" he reaches in his pocket, pulls out a piece, and says, "Here. Eat it." The first kind of teacher will say, "It has a touch of sweetness, slightly burned, sugary..." and they don't stop there. They waste paper—logs and logs and logs—trying to describe the indescribable.

A real teacher says, "You want fulfillment? Feel it. It's possible. Peace? No problem. You can have peace in your life." But when this teacher pulls out the little piece of candy and hands it to people, they say, "What's this?"

"It's the candy I'm eating. You wanted to know what it tastes like. So here, why don't you taste it for yourself?"

And then people say, "No, no!" Why? People don't know what they want.

HARD TO PLEASE
Let me illustrate with a little story. One time there was an emperor in India by the name of Akbar. There are many stories about him. He became emperor when he was quite young, and he ended up unifying India into a huge empire. Anyway, he used to hold court, and in his court, there was a courtier named Birbal who was very bright.

All the other courtiers were very jealous of Birbal, because Akbar really liked him. He always had his wits about him. One day he was late, and the emperor asked, "Where is Birbal?" The other courtiers said, "Your Majesty, he's late. He's late coming to your court!"

And they went on and on about how bad this was, until Akbar became very upset. "Why is he late? Doesn't he know I'm the emperor, and I am here, and he's not here?" and so on. By the time poor Birbal finally showed up, the emperor was furious.

"Why are you late?"

"Sire, I was taking care of my nephew. He has come to visit me, and I was taking care of him."

"Oh, so your nephew is more important than I am?" the emperor asked.

"No, sire, that's not true. But as you know, I have to take care of him, and he was being very obstinate."

152

"Anybody can satisfy a little kid!"

"If you say so, Emperor. Maybe they can, maybe they can't. I don't know."

"I'm the emperor. What is it that he would want that I could not give him?"

"I don't know, sire, if you could really appease him."

Then Akbar thought to himself, "Oh, this is good. I've got Birbal now! I've got him. With all his wit, he can't do something so simple." So he said, "Call your nephew."

When the nephew came in, a little boy about five years old, Birbal said to him, "Bow down to the emperor."

And Akbar said, "Yes, what would you like?"

The little boy answered, "I want some sugarcane."

"No problem."

The sugarcane was brought and offered to the little boy. He took the sugarcane and started crying.

"Why are you crying?" asked Akbar. "You wanted sugarcane, and I gave you sugarcane."

"I'm crying because I can't eat it. It's still got the skin on it, and it's not cut."

Akbar said, "No problem." He looked at Birbal as if to say, "You're crazy." Then he told someone to peel the sugarcane and bring it back.

So, they peeled it, cut it up, and offered it to the boy. But the boy just grabbed the bowl and started crying even louder.

"What is it now?"

The little boy said, "I've changed my mind. I want a whole one."

Akbar was still thinking, "Birbal, you made such a big deal out of this." So he gave the order: "Bring him a whole sugarcane."

The whole sugarcane was brought, and the boy started crying even louder.

Akbar said, "Why are you crying now? You wanted a sugarcane. We brought you

What does contentment feel like?

It cannot be described. It is like a mute person eating candy.

one. Then you wanted it cut. We got it cut for you. Then you changed your mind and wanted a whole one, so we brought a whole one for you. Why are you crying now?"

The boy said, "No. I don't want a *new* whole one. I want the same one that was cut to be whole."

That was when Akbar understood the words "hard to please."

We are the same way. What do we want? We don't know.

YOUR ROPE TO THE IMMORTAL
Imagine you have gone into the catacombs beneath the city of Paris. It's pitch dark, and you feed a rope behind you so you can find your way back out. You've come quite a way into the cave, and all of a sudden, even though you have been carefully laying down a line of rope, you can't find the rope anywhere. It just happened. What are you going to do?

It's common sense. You need to find the rope, because if you can do that, you can find your way back out. That's why you laid the rope down. If you suddenly realized you had dropped it somewhere, you'd stop right on the spot and search for it—and hopefully find it. And you'd say, "I got it!"

The thirst for peace and fulfillment is like that rope. Find your thirst. That is your rope to the immortal—your guide to what you have been looking for all your life and what you will be looking for the rest of your life. And what is that?

154

**Find your thirst.
That is your guide to
what you have been looking
for all your life.**

FREEDOM OR SLAVERY?

When you were young, you wanted to be older. You thought things would be better. You would be able to leave home, have your own place to live.

So you get your own place. But then you scratch your head and think, "That was just freedom from my parents. I don't quite feel free. Oh, okay. I'll get my own car. I'll get my own job. I'll become financially secure. That's it!" Off you go. You get your job, and you get set for your future.

And then you say, "What happened? I've got all this. I should be happy by now. I should be feeling free, but I feel like a slave. I have to work for this person who bosses me around all day long. All my colleagues boss me around. It's just work, work, work. Looking for freedom, I found slavery." Then you think, "Ah, *now* I know. I'll get married! Have a family." Freedom, freedom, freedom. And where do you find yourself?

You were just looking for freedom. All of a sudden it's "for better or for worse" and "till death do you part," and, "Yes, I do." And you think, "Now I'm free. I found freedom." Till you wake up the next morning and hear, "Honey..." The word *honey* is a precursor to, "Where is my breakfast?" "Why is the living room such a mess?" "Who made this mess?" "Clean up after yourself." "Be back by this time." "No, you may not. You will not; you cannot. You must not."

And then freedom becomes, "Baby, baby, baby! I want to have a baby!"

So you go through the fun part. Soon there's a baby in a sort of sac below the stomach. Everything is fine, and you think, "So cute. Yes, we'll have our own football team or our own hockey team, and we'll do this and we'll do that. We'll go out there and we'll accomplish this and . . ." Then baby arrives.

There you are. You've had a long day, especially the mother. She would like some rest, but men usually feel they have had just about as long a day.

And the baby? Of course, the baby doesn't have a clock or a watch. "Waaah. Waaaah."

"Honey, go check on the baby."

"What? Whaaat?"

And then? Promotion, promotion, promotion. Money means freedom. A promotion comes, but by the time it does, there has been so much inflation that you've actually been financially demoted. You are more in debt than you could have ever imagined.

156

Now, don't mistake me. I'm not against having babies or families or finding a job and all that, but put it in perspective. Why do you want a family? Why do you want a job? Why do you want to move out of the house? Don't do it under false pretenses, because when you do that, guess who will be the most disappointed? You.

Meanwhile, ever since this freedom business began, and even before that, something has been sharpening its knife, waiting for you. Do you want to know the definition of patience? *Time*. Time has patience. It waits.

It's hyper-intelligent, sees absolutely no difference between a beggar, a king, an emperor. To time, everyone is the same.

WHAT IF GOD WAS LISTENING?
Today, people pray for everything. I think they've got Santa Claus and God mixed up. On TV, I saw soldiers praying before they went out to fight. "God, give me strength to kill all my enemies." Can you imagine if the enemy was also praying? "God, give me the strength to mow down my enemies." And God's probably laughing. "They're both asking for the same thing."

What if God was listening? Is that really what you want to say? Imagine that the maker of the universe, the creator of time, the infinite is listening—just to you. What would you say? "Make me pass my exams." Really? "Give me a longer life." Really? "Make me a richer man." Really? I mean, really?

Think about it. The creator of every speck of dust and every star, who will be there long after human beings have been erased by time, is listening to you. What would you like to say?

Let me put it more in context. Imagine that your spouse has been in the hospital in a deep coma for a long time. The doctors have predicted that he or she will come out of the coma for five seconds. Just five seconds. And then after that, your spouse will be gone forever.

What would you like to say? You have tons of questions, but you love this person very much. You have five seconds. That's all. Just five seconds. What would you say? "Honey, uh, where is that lawn mower you bought?" "I was wondering where the latest will is." Really?

If it were me, I would boil it down to what matters the most. Forget about the lawn mower. Forget about the will. Forget about where the keys to the house are.

All I would say is, "I love you." Not, "We've only got five seconds. Do you love me?" No. "I love you."

Seek the immortal.
It resides in you.
It always has, always will.

GRATITUDE

There's a very simple reality when everything is boiled down to what is important in life. And if my God were hearing me, the only thing I would like to say is, "Thank you."

There is an amazing grace in the life of every human being. But maybe you look at your life, and you see in it what *isn't*. I suggest you start to look at your life and see what *is*. Maybe you look at your existence and make a list of all the things you do *not* have.

I suggest you start to see the things you *do* have. Maybe you look at all the things you have *not* achieved. I suggest you start to see the things you *have* achieved. And that is not about psychology or pumping you up to make you feel good. The achievement I am talking about is the breath. It's a miracle.

Do you like miracles as a sideshow, or do you like real miracles? If you like miracles as a sideshow, you will have to work very hard for them. But if you like the real miracles, then just look at your breath. It is an incredible miracle that is taking place every moment of your life.

158

TRANQUILITY IN A VIOLENT UNIVERSE

I talk to a lot of people. And many people seem to have a bubble around them—their ideas about what everything is. They exist in this sphere, totally isolated, unfortunately, from reality. And they protect their bubble, fearing that what's outside of it is terrible, horrible.

The reality is quite different. What's outside the sphere, what the reality really is, is gorgeous, beautiful, incredible. It's real. It changes, it dances, it moves, it inspires. And it's your reality. Yours.

Who are you? What is this life all about? If I were to say, "It's about you," would you believe it?

HOSTILE UNIVERSE

I was watching a video from a TV series about the universe. They were showing that the universe is very hostile. Things are always exploding: planets, stars. Huge heavenly bodies are being decimated, and these explosions stretch over light years. Earth is a speck of dust in comparison.

Outside of this Earth, supersonic winds are being radiated from the sun, and Earth is being blasted by them. Here, if there are fifty-mile-an-hour winds, people say, "Wow, it's windy!" Here, people are concerned about getting too many X-rays because of radiation. Out there, there's so much radiation that if you left the surface of Earth, you'd get cooked on the spot. Literally.

And yet, have you ever looked at the stars in the night sky and said, "It's so beautiful, so serene, so tranquil"? See, this life is about you. You've been placed on this earth, and you have been isolated from the forces of the universe because you couldn't handle them. You would die. You'd vanish. But for this period called a *lifetime*, everything has been put in proportion for you, so you can actually look out and not see the violence, but see tranquility.

WHAT IS A HUMAN GOOD FOR?

And then, take a look at what's happening with you. You create your own violence. You create your own turmoil. You don't need anybody else to do that. You just need your own misunderstanding of what life is about. You take what is so obvious and utterly destroy its obviousness, making it mysterious and distant. That power, that energy, whose nature is peace, whose nature is joy, is so approachable—and you make it so unapproachable.

If you put a chili into a frying pan with hot oil in it, the chili is going to get fried. The nature of the frying pan is that it'll conduct the heat and keep the oil from running down into the fire. It holds the oil and the chili, and it conducts the heat through the metal to the oil. The oil's nature is to hold the heat, and the chili's nature is to fry when it comes in contact with hot oil. Isn't that simple? Isn't that clear?

So. What is *your* nature? Your nature is that when you come in contact with that power that's inside of you, joy springs forth, peace happens.

Now, what else is a frying pan good for? You could hit somebody over the head with it, and it would be an effective weapon, I suppose. But that's not what the frying pan was built for. You could possibly use a frying pan to dig a hole, but that's not what it was built for. You could try to use a frying pan as a hat—put it on your head and walk around holding the handle. It would work, but that's not what it was built for. So if you are wondering what a frying pan is good for, the answer is obvious—for frying, heating. That's what it's built for.

So then the question becomes, what's a human being good for? What were you built for? Fighting wars? No. Why? You get killed. Destroyed.

What *is* a human being good for? When you take a deeper look at it, you understand that the human body is the vessel through which peace and joy can be attained. And what you do in your life to attain that is the proper use of this human body. Everything else you do that does not bring you joy and does not bring you peace, is not what this body was made for.

DESTRUCTION

Now, that's a very big statement and I'm sure there are people who'll say, "Well, you've got to have your job, and you've got to earn money so you can have a house and all those things and take care of all your responsibilities." Excuse me. Let's get some facts down first. How many coins does it take to make a mango tree grow? And how many coins does it take to put a mango on the branch? We live in a system that somebody created, but there was a time when this system didn't exist. If people felt hungry, they went out, gathered food, and ate it. Somewhere along the evolution of human beings, the idea of ownership came about. Before that, it would have been, "Own what?" What people ate was grass. Wheat is basically grass, but over a long period of time, human beings have cultivated and modified it. Before that, it grew wherever it grew, and people went and gathered it. And they survived just fine. That's why we are here today.

And not only are we here, but now our ego is so big that we look at those people—our ancestors—and say, "Oh, I wasn't like that." Yes, you were. And the bad news—or the good news—is you still are. This civilized society is far closer to the brink of extinction than were the ones we call *primitive*. They survived on this earth for a much longer period of time than we have as this civilized society where everywhere you turn, one country after another is justifying destruction.

With a frying pan, you can at least dig a hole. With some of these modern weapons, you can't do anything with them but destroy. And we think about all this. But our reasoning is not used for peace. Absolutely not. Our reasoning is used to rationalize wars. Utter destruction. Our creative power is not used for something beautiful; it is used to create weapons that are supposed to decimate faster, quicker, better, and, as we are told, "with great precision." What do you mean by "precision"? Precisely what? You're talking about destruction. When the bomb blows, it blows. Indiscriminately. Now, that's the situation in the world.

But what I have to say is not about what's going on in the world. It's about what's going on in your life. It's about what you see, what you feel. Do you feel your heart? Do you feel a passion for peace in your life? Do you feel a passion for joy, contentment, understanding, clarity in your life?

162

What's a human being good for? Fighting wars? No. Why? You get killed.

OBEY WHAT?

What drives you every day? Is it all your reasoning—"But I have to, I have to, I have to"—or is it the desire from deep within you to be fulfilled? Because if you listen to that desire, if you acknowledge that in your life, then it becomes your companion. It becomes the force that shapes you, that evolves you, that turns you toward what you were made for.

Ultimately, the main question is, "In this life, what do you have to do?" You are here for a very short period of time, an extremely short period. And as you were growing up, there was a part of you that was simple and innocent, trying to enjoy. That's all you cared about. Then, all too soon, you were being taught "responsibility."

It was not that you were irresponsible. You understood responsibility very well. But you thought that your responsibility was to have a good time. Whatever it took to do that was what you had to do. That was your agenda. Then you were taught, "No, no, no. You must learn to obey others. If you can learn that, then you will be a good, responsible person."

Now that you've grown up, you hate this idea. When somebody tells you, "You have to obey," you don't want to. You see street signs that post the speed limit at fifty-five miles per hour or seventy or eighty kilometers, and you don't like that. You want to go the speed you want to go. You want to do what you want to do. That is the biggest illusion there is.

Why is that the biggest illusion? Because you already have been told to obey, and it is ingrained in you. From morning till evening, you obey, and obey, and obey. What you don't obey is what your heart is trying to tell you—to feel free.

Why is it that the idea of freedom, the word freedom, is so appealing? Because you know intrinsically that you're not free. You have learned to live within the walls; you have learned to obey. And now it's ingrained in you.

THE HEART IS YOUR MESSIAH

There is something that happens every day of your life. The sweet, sweet beautiful breath comes into you. It comes in and goes out, comes in and goes out, all the while bringing you the abundance of existence, consciousness, awareness.

If you can be aware that you are alive, that you exist, then, even though there is unbelievable violence in the universe not that far away, here on the face of this earth, for *you* there can be unbelievable tranquility and beauty.

When you can feel that the coming and going of this breath is the blessing in your existence, that's the day you become free. That's the real freedom. That is the day you will say, "I have been blessed. All my prayers have been answered."

In every religion they say, "The messiah is going to come"—their own messiah. What if God said, "All right, all you messiahs, out of here. Go down there at the same time"? Do you realize what a mess that would be?

Could you consider the possibility that the messiah, in the form of a heart, has already been placed within every single human being? And whose message does this heart give? Do you really expect a messiah to come and pick up the *Bhagavad Gita* and say, "Let me quote this"? People would say, "We've already read that." If a messiah picked up a Bible and said, "Let me read to you chapter three, verse four," people would scratch their heads and say, "What kind of messiah is that?" And if the messiah said, "Forget about that and let me tell you something new," they would all say, "But he doesn't quote from scripture. What kind of messiah is this?" I think that's what happens to messiahs. Then they go up to heaven, and God says, "You want to go back down?" and they all say, "No!"

If a messiah *volunteered* to go down, even God would say, "Man, you're really dumb. Didn't you learn the first time? They hacked you to death, they nailed you to a cross, they did this to you, they did all that to you, and you want to go down there?"

Why would anybody want to repeat that? But the messiah you're looking for is here in the form of your heart—and has always been here. And what this messiah speaks of is what you need. This messiah speaks of joy, of tranquility, of peace to help you understand the importance of every single day of your life—to help you understand the importance of being alive, to help you understand the importance of the thirst inside of you to be content, to recognize that beauty again and again and again.

People are allured by heaven, but you are in heaven here. Your god resides within you, and by virtue of that, your heaven is within you. You look for truth. The truth is that you are alive. The truth is that you exist. The truth is that you can feel peace. The truth is that you can feel clarity in your life—that is the truth, *your* truth. And the day you understand that, you *will* be saved.

**Everywhere you turn,
one country after another
is justifying destruction.**

When you come in contact with that power that's inside of you —joy springs forth, peace happens.

Saved from what? What do you need saving from? You need to be saved from unconsciousness. You need to be saved from confusion. You need to be saved from doubt. These are your enemies. These are the elements that eat away at you because they rob you of the presence of knowing your existence. These are the things that make you forget you are alive.

Take away the confusion and unconsciousness, and the pain and suffering will be gone, because the day you begin to acknowledge your life, you begin to understand that this life is the blessing.

And in this incredible, magnificent creation, this garden has been created. Superb. What an incredible garden it is!

One of the songs of Kabir says, "He has created everything that needs a foundation. And yet, in itself, it needs no foundation. He is away from all his creation, and yet he is in every fiber of that creation."

How sweet. How beautiful. It is there but not obtrusive. It is present but invisible. Even what cannot be seen with these eyes is present in the eyes. *These* are your truths. *These* are your realities that you need to embrace every day. And that's what clarity is.

RELIGIONS
Do you have clarity in your life? There's a saying in aviation: "The outcome of any maneuver should never be in question." Is your life like that—that the outcome of whatever you're doing shall never be in question? I don't think so. We like to take our chances. "What are you doing?" "I don't know. Let's hope for the best."

People pray for a lot of things. Anything happens, "Let's pray." These days, it's absolutely incredible. They're saying, "Let's go kill all these people." And they actually pray to God that they kill them all successfully.

Do they think God has forgotten about everything? He went on a vacation, slipped on the floor, hit his head on something, and now has no clue that we're even here on planet Earth, that there's nobody really looking after us, so we need to constantly ring his bell and say, "This and this, and this, and this…"

What if a pilot said, "Ladies and gentlemen, this is your captain speaking. Welcome aboard Flight such-and-such. Right now, we really need to pray to God that he will help us reach that magical fifty feet above the runway as we take off. This airplane has just been in maintenance. So, will you please join me, close your eyes, and pray: 'God, we really need your help today to get off the ground, so please help us. Amen.'"

If I heard that, I wouldn't care about the consequences. I'd open the emergency exit and step out of that airplane. I shouldn't do that; they'd put me in jail. But, hey, it's okay. At least I wouldn't be on that airplane.

I really don't have any problem with religions. My only problem is when people start fighting over them. Because whenever war happens, who suffers the most? Innocent people who had nothing to do with it. They lead simple lives; they are innocent. They work on their fields, get enough food for two meals a day, and are satisfied. Yet they're the ones who get killed every time.

People try to legitimize war: "That's a good war" or "That's a legit war." And this is what I don't like—to make people fight with each other in the name of God. That's just plain wrong. Right now, all the religions should be among the foremost proponents of peace. Uncompromisingly. All the religions should be united behind one cause: peace and prosperity for all people. But they've become the dividing lines.

What is this life all about? If I were to say, "It's about you," would you believe it?

167

What's going to happen because of this? It's only going to escalate. I know there are hundreds and hundreds of millions of people who just want to live in peace. They want a little elbow room. They want to be left alone. They just want to exist and enjoy their lives. They're willing to take their plows and plow their fields and grow some vegetables. This is fine with them. There are a lot of people like that. They're not looking for handouts. Don't want them. A simple life is good enough for them. But they are not going to be left alone. Why?

YOUR REALITY

Do you pray to God in troubled times? What does God say? "Find your peace, find your contentment, find your joy." What does God say if you pray in good times? "Find your peace, find your contentment, find your joy." You want to pray, but you don't accept God's replies. How does God reply? "You're fortunate. You are alive. Here is my blessing. My blessing to you is this breath." Do you accept that? Do you prepare yourself for this blessing every day?

What is the reality? You are alive. That's the reality. What's going to happen tomorrow? Don't worry. Something will happen. There are two possibilities: one, you might die. If you die, you don't have to worry about tomorrow because you'll be gone. If you don't show up for your job because you're dead, and your boss says, "Why did that person do that?" you don't have to answer. Even if you have a lot of unpaid parking tickets, it's okay. It's not like they're going to chase after you. It's over.

The other possibility is that you'll be alive. And you *can* do something about that. You can prepare to greet tomorrow with consciousness, with clarity, with understanding, with a heart full of joy.

WE WERE BORN AND FELL ASLEEP

You cannot help but feel that for a lot of people there is a struggle in life. We struggle with so many things. Why? Whenever you have two forces opposing each other, you have a struggle. And to resolve the struggle, first you have to identify what those two elements are. Once you have identified them, you can choose which one you want and then take away what you do not want.

So, what are the elements in our lives that most commonly cause us to struggle? How does this struggle come to be?

Hundreds of years ago, a poet said that we were born and then we fell asleep. Take it for what it's worth. I know there's a lot of skepticism toward such a thought. But whatever your reality may be, entertain this thought for just a minute—that we were born and we fell asleep. And in this sleep, we experience all the traumas of this world, all the laughter—everything. So, imagine a person is asleep, and sometimes the person laughs, sometimes the person cries, sometimes the person screams, and sometimes the person speaks. It's like having a nightmare again and again. And yet, there is a great desire to keep on dreaming, because the dream becomes so intoxicating that you want to stay asleep.

To entertain the possibility that we need to wake up is truly very difficult for us. If you go into the street right now and say to somebody, "You are asleep. Would you like to wake up?" they would look at you like, "Are you crazy?" Not only are we asleep, but we *like* that state of being asleep. We are used to it. We don't understand what it would mean to be awake.

So when somebody comes and says, "Wake up," it sounds peculiar. You are so caught up in the dream that you don't understand why somebody would say this. "What do you mean, 'wake up'? I *am* awake. Isn't this all real? All the good, the bad, the traumas—everything that happens in this world—isn't that real?"

How many of us have experienced a flat tire and the frustration it brings? How many of us have burned something we were cooking or ripped our pants accidentally and felt so embarrassed? And when you feel that, doesn't it seem real? And yet, what is the *consequence* of all these things that happen to us? Not much. Another day comes and you move on.

Could it be true, then, that everything that happens in our state of dreaming while awake is of little consequence?

WAKING UP
We do not understand the dynamic of being asleep and being awake. But somebody comes to say, "Wake up," and what they are saying is that there is something you can do that *will* have a consequence in your lives—not a negative consequence, but a positive one.

There are people who do not understand that life is a gift. They can't. They are constantly torn between their wishes and how everything actually unfolds in their lives. They're caught in a terrible, terrible nightmare. And they are not the only ones dreaming. Everybody is dreaming.

We are in other people's dreams, and they are in ours. In *our* dream, we see somebody pass away, and in their dream, they see us being left on this earth as they move on. And it pains us when we look into the future and realize, "Now I will be without

170

Somebody comes and says, "Wake up!"

You are so caught up in the dream that you say, "I am awake. Isn't this all real?"

this person." The present doesn't pain us. The future does. Memories come from the past: "Oh, this was a wonderful person," and you know, that may not have been true. You might've hated that person, but now that they're gone, you look into the future and say, "Now all the good things that might have happened won't happen, and so it's going to be very, very painful."

What are the consequences, then, of being awake? *Awakening* means to accept the beautiful reality that you are alive. You look, you observe, you see, you understand. And you build, because every step you take has a positive consequence.

When you are asleep, time is only relative to what is going to happen. Maybe you are waiting for someone to pick you up and take you to the airport. You look at your watch and think, "Okay, I have four minutes left; I have three minutes left; I have two minutes left. Now I have to go." What the clock really is telling you is, "Here goes another second of life. Here goes another minute of life. Here goes another hour of life." But those who are sleeping don't understand this. Only the awake can understand the importance of the time they are given.

Do you understand today? Do you understand now? Do you understand that this time has been given to you? To *you*! That should mean *everything*. The concept of today, the concept of *now,* can never be understood if you are asleep. But when you are awake, you understand what it means to have today, to have now.

TIRED TRAVELER
I often say, "This life is a gift." I'm not talking about what you get for Christmas or your birthday or the things you give to other people. How can you compare life with those things? It's not an object that you can buy at a store, wrap in a pretty piece of paper, and hand to somebody with a note that says "Thank you," or "Happy birthday," or "I got you this." Life is *priceless*. Do you know what *priceless* means? Have you ever actually come across anything that was priceless?

171

Every breath is priceless. Life is above and beyond any value that we can measure. Every day is incredibly valuable. Every moment that you exist and are conscious is incredibly valuable. Does being *conscious* mean being awake? You bet. That's exactly what it means.

As we sleep, lullabies abound and the bed is soft. And, of course, the traveler is tired. Why? Because the traveler started traveling but didn't know where to go. So the traveler has gone up one road and come back. Gone up another one and come back. Gone up another one and come back. We live our lives with trials: "Well, let's try it and see where it goes."

And when it doesn't work out? Back we come, and off we go again. What can you understand when you don't even know that you are lost?

So, awakening becomes tremendously important. And, believe me, awakening is not going to be part of your dream. You won't dream about being awakened. Awakening will only happen when somebody comes and says, "Awaken." And what will many people say? "I *am* awake." Or "Why?" Or "Who is this?"

But there is something in you that wants to awaken—that's what causes the struggle. One part wants to sleep, and the other part wants to wake up.

DUST TO DUST
So, awaken and realize what this life is. And know that all that you find so magical, all that you find so incredible in this world are elements that have been derived from dust. And they have an innate propensity to turn back into dust—that's what they do. This body of yours constantly sheds skin. The younger you are, the more it sheds. The older you are, the less it sheds.

To have clarity in your life, you have to remove all that doesn't belong there and causes you to struggle.

The process of dust-to-dust is happening while you are alive. You don't even have to die. Dust-to-dust is afoot. In the universe, there is a tremendous amount of dust whirling around. And once in a while, this dust is packed up and turns into a planet. This earth was made out of dust, and one day, it will become dust again. By the very nature of everything around you, this is what you are and this is what your world is: Dust, dust, and more dust. Except for *one* thing.

The thirst to feel the most beautiful, the possibility to feel the most beautiful, and the most beautiful itself are the only elements in you that are not part of the dust. Everything else is destined to go toward dust, is going toward dust, and will go toward dust. You can bank on that.

"WORD OF GOD"
So, if you want to be mesmerized, be mesmerized by the most beautiful that is inside of you. The thirst to feel the most beautiful does not reside in your mind or in your thoughts. It resides in your heart. That's why you need to listen to your heart.

The mind likes to chase itself, so it says, "Think about the unthinkable. Comprehend the incomprehensible. Try to see the unseeable. Try to hear the inaudible. Try to grab the infinite. Try to time the timeless." Around and around and around it goes.

Every religion is trying to define the indefinable. And people fight over their religion. Every religion says, "This is the word of God. This is the final version; there are no more versions after this." Some people are proud and say, "This is the original version." Others say, "No, that is the second version; it was revised." It's like software revisions: version 1.0, 2.0, 3.0, and so on.

Do you understand what is actually being said in all the "words of God"? That "the kingdom of heaven is within"? That what you are looking for is within you? This you'll find in every single version.

In reality, God speaks to everyone every single day. The voice of the heart is saying, "Be fulfilled. Be in joy. Be in beauty. Feel the most beautiful. Understand, accept. Be in clarity. Don't be in doubt."

Have you ever wondered why pain is painful and why joy is joyful? It's simple. Joy is supposed to be. Pain is not.

Clarity is not something strange. Clarity resides in every single human being. You don't need another person for it; believe me. To have clarity in your life, you have to be able to remove all the things that don't belong there and that cause you to struggle. That's all.

What is tomorrow?

The big illusion
that everybody believes in.

HEAVEN IS WITHIN

Is it possible to spend every day fulfilled? It is. Does it take some doing? Yes, it does. Being conscious is not easy, especially if your habit is to fall asleep or if your habit is to be unconscious. But is it possible? Yes.

You can suffer so much pain in your life because of one second of unconsciousness. One second of unconsciousness can have devastating effects. If you look at the cost of the two, the difference is striking: one second of consciousness is cheap compared to the possibility of an entire lifetime of agony and pain.

What is tomorrow? The big illusion that everybody believes in. Some people are waiting for the day they're going to ascend to heaven. What I am saying is that there is a heaven within us. Ascend, then, to the heaven inside of you. While you are alive.

LIGHT OR LAMPS?

There is so much that distracts us from now, so much that distracts us from our reality. Are you seeking to remove your thirst, or are you seeking to quench your thirst? It's a very pointed question. Say you are thirsty, and you are in a desert. You come across an oasis, and there are two ponds. One pond is labeled "Drink this water, and you will never feel thirsty again." And the other one says, "If you want to quench your thirst, please feel free to do so." Which one are you going to go for? Puzzled?

You might be thinking, "Yes, I want my thirst removed forever." Well, there is one way that can happen. If the water in the first pond is poisonous, then you will die if you drink it, and you'll never feel thirsty again. The other one is very simple. The point of it is not that you should never be thirsty again. If you're going to live, you *are* going to be thirsty. The point is that whenever you are thirsty, you should have access to water so that you can quench your thirst.

Many people think that once you get "enlightened," that's it. The bulb is *on.* No. The enlightened one has his or her relationship with light, not with the bulb. So if there is plenty of light outside, turn off the lamp. Not needed. And when it gets dark, then light the lamp. The relationship is not with the lamp; it's with the light. You have been chasing lamps. So you have many lamps but no light. And that's the condition of the world—plenty of lamps but no light.

175

There are some who call themselves masters, who are masters of lamps—not of light but of lamps. They have old lamps, new lamps, fancy lamps, and very sedate lamps.

There are people who carry their lamps but never light them. They carry their lamps unlit in the night because something might happen to the lamp if it got lit, and they want to protect it. So they get bruised, because their hands aren't free to protect themselves as they fall. They just keep falling and being bruised.

I've been called a master by some people. It has made virtually no difference in my life. If nobody called me a master, that would be fine with me. If somebody calls me a master, that is fine, too. Do I see myself as a master? No. But I do have a relationship with light. I really don't care about the lamps.

WHAT IS PEACE?
There are people who believe that there cannot be peace. And then there are people like me who believe that there can be peace. I just want to say one thing to you: This world belongs to the believers. Historically, that's how it has been. When they said, "Let's put a man on the moon," there were nonbelievers and believers. Nonbelievers don't have to work out solutions. All they have to do is point out the impossibility. Believers look for solutions. To them, there is no obstacle so big that it cannot be removed. If it needs to be overcome, they find a way to overcome it. That's how it needs to happen with peace.

Maybe you have five reasons why there cannot be peace. Maybe you have ten reasons why there cannot be peace, such as there's too much greed, too much politics, too many armies. Whatever. Ten reasons? Fifteen? Twenty? I say there are 6.7 billion reasons why there should be peace on this earth—because there are 6.7 billion people alive today. And each human being on the face of this earth is a reason why there should be peace.

But most people don't understand what peace is. They've never tasted it, never been around it; they've just heard about it. They think that the absence of war is peace, but war is only a symptom.

Here is an analogy: You have a cold, so you go to the doctor.

The doctor says, "What's wrong with you?"

You say, "My nose is running."

The doctor says, "Okay, let's stop it." And he shoves two corks up your nose. "Now it's not running anymore!"

Then you say, "My throat is sore."

176

Something in you wants to awaken— that's what causes the struggle.

One part wants to sleep; the other part wants to wake up.

And he says, "Well, when do you feel the soreness?"

"Every time I swallow."

"Then don't swallow!"

Needless to say, nobody wants such a doctor. But that's how we approach peace. Stopping the wars isn't going to bring peace. Wars have been stopped many times— but they have a way of restarting. If there is a fire, and you just keep putting out little sparks here and there, the fire will start up again and again because the source of the fire has not been extinguished.

A lot of people paint peace as a vegetative state. Once you have it, you become totally undynamic. It's equivalent to having a lobotomy. That's not peace. A person with peace is dynamic! Because they're alive. They're not sleeping; they're alive. They look forward to the blessing of the breath as it comes in and out. They want to feel thankful every day, every second that they can. Peace is dynamic. Living life is dynamic. And that's how it should be for you. Dynamic. Living. Existing.

WONDERMENT
Many people don't wonder anymore. The extent of their wonderment is, "Why is the traffic moving so slow?" And the city government has even taken that privilege away by putting up signs saying "Accident ahead." So, now you know why the traffic is moving so slow. And people are just bored. Don't be bored. Not one second should you be bored if you understand what life is about. Wherever you go, wherever you are, turn within. Understand. Wonder.

We really have an opportunity in life. And it's not to struggle. That's not how life should be. Understanding and admiring—that's how your life should be, regardless of what happens. Not projections into the future. Not memories of the past. But to be awake and enjoy life. As far as I am concerned, if, in the truest sense of the word, you can enjoy one day, you've done well. You've done really well.

There will be nothing like
this home of existence ever again.

YOUR HOME OF EXISTENCE

This is an analogy I thought about when I was coming back home from a tour. What is a home? We've all heard sayings like "Home sweet home" and "Welcome home." But what is a home?

If you are lucky, that is where you will take your last breath—if you don't get mowed down by a truck or fall out of an airplane into the heart of the Amazon jungle or in the middle of an ocean.

Listen to what the heart has to say.
It is not a big philosophy.
It is not a big drum.
It is a very short statement
that says, "Be content."

Home is a place where sometimes there is turmoil, and yet there is also incredible comfort to be had. This is where, hopefully, you have cultivated a happy environment where you can thrive, where you're not inundated with problems. It is truly a place of comfort—not only physical comfort, but also mental comfort and the comfort of knowing that you are at home.

How can this home be a home? You have to work on it. I am not referring to deciding which direction the door faces or how fancy it is. I have seen happiness and comfort in a hut. It might be built out of mud, with a dry, thatched roof and a little door that doesn't even have locks on it, but the people who live there are comfortable. When you see this, you understand that, for them, it is not a matter of which way their door faces. They live there, and that is what is important to them.

YOUR 15 MINUTES

So, why am I talking about home? Because this existence is your home. And it is incumbent upon you to make this home as comfortable as possible, as peaceful as possible, as beautiful as possible, as real as possible. Because this home of existence is where the truest nurturing takes place. In this home of existence, good things happen and bad things happen, but you have to make sure that the good things happen by nurturing them, by bringing forward the true joy that this home can offer.

There will be nothing like this home of existence ever again. It is hard to believe, isn't it? It is hard to believe that you will be allowed only 15 minutes on this most magnificent stage, and then the curtains will close, you will be asked to leave, and somebody else will come. And there will be another and another and another.

For most people, it is extremely hard to believe that there is no more. I say to people who have lost someone close to them, "It's okay. They've not gone anywhere; they're still with you. They live in your memories. You, being alive, can see them; you can feel them; you can think about them. They dance with you. They are with you. And the companionship may not be the same, but it continues to unfold. Nurture that. Understand that. Because in that, there is no shame, and there is no agony. It is the nature of things."

It's like when water flows—this is when water is happy. It can once again begin to play with life. It can once again harbor other life forms. When the water is static, it dies.

Do you know how water dies? It's amazing. On one hand, you have fresh water. If it becomes landlocked, it becomes saltier and saltier, until everything in it begins to die. On the other hand, you have an incredible ocean, and it is salty, but in it, life flourishes. And all that the sweet, fresh water wants is to go back into the ocean and become salty again. That is its best chance of becoming pure and clean once again. That's its best chance to purge itself of every impurity. It has no other way. And so it babbles, and it rushes to return once again to where it came from.

THE CHALLENGE

Understand that your nature is like that water; don't fight it. Don't ask, "Why?" Because your "Why?" will never be answered. Ever. You try to reason, but what you use to reason is the most unreasonable, because it cannot understand.

People make discoveries. And they say, "Wow! We discovered this!" Do you understand how foolish that must look to Nature? Nature must think, "I knew about this before you were even a glint in your parents' eyes." We reason with the unreasonable. We try to understand that which cannot be understood. And we define the indefinable.

We, the living, act like the dead—impervious to all that is happening around us, impervious to the most magnificent thing that is happening within us. This breath, this gift, this gentleness comes to us; life unfolds effortlessly for us. We don't have to pull on a rope. We don't have to push a button. It unfolds.

And in this time that you have, this consciousness, this opportunity to know—what have you come to know? What have you understood?

This existence is your home. Make it as comfortable as possible, as peaceful as possible, as beautiful as possible, as real as possible.

The challenge before us is to understand the obvious. How do you understand the obvious? Listen to what the heart has to say. It is not a big philosophy. It is not a big drum. It is a very short statement that says, "Be content."

Could there be a miracle in just acceptance—that I simply accept my existence and something great will happen? Yes, that's what I'm talking about. That's the obvious. It's right there. Accept the breath that you have been given.

THE GNOSTICS

I was watching a TV documentary. It was about the Gospel of Judas. It talks a little bit about Judas, and then it suggests that there was a lot more going on in early

182

Christianity than people have been led to believe. A professor talked about the Nag Hammadi scrolls from the Gnostics and explained what they are about.

He said, "These people believed in a knowledge that did not come from any book. They believed that in every human being dwells the spark of the same God and that they could feel it. They would sit down and achieve a tranquil state with their eyes closed." Amazing. Why? Because there were some people who understood something a long time ago, and that spark is not dead even today, when virtually everything else has changed.

What people want to believe in, how they want to believe in it, and so many other things have changed. But one thing has not changed: the quest for the spark of the divine that dwells in the heart of every human being. That we look for it and want to feel it today is no different than it was two thousand years ago.

So it's important to make this home of existence as beautiful as you can. And you really have to work on it. Garbage must go out. Begin with getting the garbage out and resolving not to bring more garbage in.

Both have to happen simultaneously. Because if you make the resolution to throw out the garbage and don't resolve to not bring it back in, you're going to throw it out and bring it back in, throw it out and bring it back in. This is what we all do. This is why we don't learn. We make mistakes, and we swear up and down, "I have learned my lesson." But the only lesson you have learned is how to forget the lessons you have learned.

YOUR FUNERAL

So things creep along, and you forget, thinking, "Ha-ha. Everything is wonderful. I'm the king; I'm the boss; this is my little world." Hey. We're talking about home. Your home. We're not talking about the world. But you think, "Everything is fine now. Everything is great. I did this; I have to do that. I'm important." This is what you want to know—that the world thinks the world of you. How many times have you been through this cycle, where you feel so important, and then you come to understand that the world really doesn't care about you or think the world of you? It doesn't even know you exist.

Even if somebody takes you and puts you in prison, you get to bring your home along.

183

Believe me, the people who show up at your funeral do not show up because of you. You know that, right? They actually show up because of everybody else who is still around. You'll be gone. You won't even know who showed up.

How do I know they come because of other people and not you? Because when the button is pushed and you are buried, they go have a party, and you will not be invited. And if you showed up at that party, they'd freak out! That's how it is. They're going to talk about you until they're halfway through the first drink. Then, as alcohol is absorbed into the bloodstream, you may come up once in a while in the midst of the conversation, but it's mostly going to be about, "So, what do you do?"

We live in a world that is full of hypocrisy. And that's not the worst part. The worst part is, we're all members of that group. We actually help perpetuate that stuff. Begin to understand the reality of this home of existence. It is so unbelievably fragile. I can't even tell you how fragile it is. And yet, it is the very place that will protect you from the storms, from the lightning, from the hurricanes, from the hail. It is so delicate and yet so strong that it is almost unbelievable.

A HAPPY HOME

And you think all you have to do is decorate it to make it look good? No. Decoration is okay, but first make sure it is a happy home. Because if a home is happy, it doesn't matter if it is decorated. If it is, good; but first, it has to be a happy home.

So what have you done lately to make your home a happy home? And what do you plan to do tomorrow? What music will play there? What lights will illuminate it? Will clean water flow through and around this home? Will fresh air come through it? How simple will this home be?

When was the last time you really opened the windows to this home without being fearful of what might come in? When did you last feel safe to leave the door open? When did you last turn on the lights and look around? When did you last sit down and admire this home and feel thankful for having a home?

How does that saying go? "Be it ever so humble, there's no place like home." Of course, good days will come and bad days will come. That's why you need to make sure your home is in good shape. Because this home is yours. No mortgage. No liens. No loans. This one is yours. And it is yours in such a beautiful way—nobody can take it away from you till the very last breath.

Even if somebody takes you and puts you in prison, you get to bring your home along. If you have never taken care of this home, then you will be homeless. Even if you have everything, you will not have a home. The day you find your home, you will realize you can live without a lot of things, because you have a home.

In this home of existence, find the spark of the divine and make that your companion.

There are all these tragedies and problems in the world. I know it's hard. But they are not about you. This home is about you. And your home should be the most beautiful home, not in comparison to others, but the best for you, so you have no qualms living in this home, and when you are there, you really feel at home. You feel fortunate to have such a home.

HERE I AM

In this home of existence, find the spark of the divine and make that your companion. It is a great blessing when you begin to see the good. The good. The beauty of something as it is meant to be. You understand the perfection of how things are. You understand why the water is in such a rush. The next time you see a flowing river, smile. Next time you see a waterfall, smile, because you just understood where the water is headed.

The day you begin to truly pursue understanding, in that one second when you see that water relentlessly flowing day and night—you have just read a scripture. And you have not only read a scripture, you have understood it! You got it without 15,000 people trying to explain to you what it really means.

When a flower starts to bloom in January, a lot of people call it a "false start." It isn't really. The flower is not looking at the calendar; it is not looking at a clock. It's just being there. There is something it has waited for and waited for and waited for. And now the time has come. Its relationship is not with the calendar. Its relationship is with temperature. When the right temperature comes, it says, "Here I am."

Your life is a story that begins with "Here I am." And why are you here? You are here because the spark of the divine is in you, and the blessing of breath comes in and goes out. That is the core.

To survive the crises of this world, you're going to need your home, and you're going to need your feet. You're going to have to learn how to stand on your own feet. It may be painful, but it's a good thing. At least it will be your feet you will be standing on, not somebody else's.

You will also need strength, and it will have to be inner strength, not the outer one. That's not going to help you. It might help you push shopping carts, but the one you need is inner strength.

SOMETHING IS AFOOT

Awakening is a very gentle, beautiful process, not jarring like a thunderstorm. Awakening is not like getting shocked with one of those resuscitators on your chest that bring you back from death. That's what people think awakening is. You've got a 200,000-volt thing going, "Grrrrrr! Grrrrr!" and your body is screaming, "I'm awake!" That's not what awakening is. Awakening is a very gentle, beautiful process. It's like grass that comes up through the earth and grows just a little at a time. You can't tell when it happened, but the next thing you know, it's there. A flower, a seed. Sprouting.

Have you ever looked at waves? You look out at the ocean, and there's nothing there; it all looks flat. Then a wave starts to come closer and closer, building and building, until the next thing you know, white water hits the shore.

And then you look out a few thousand feet behind the waves, and nothing is happening there. Where are they coming from? Ah! Something is afoot way out there.

Maybe the only place you get to see it is right at the shoreline, but this process has been afoot for thousands of miles. This wave that you just saw breaking in front of you didn't just start here. It's been traveling, traveling, traveling. The next time you see a wave, understand that. This little thing started way out there.

You, too, are a traveler. Where are you going? "I'm just going. I'm bound by that nature." Understand that. Don't question it. Are you pointless? Are you going to bang against that shore and disappear? Ah! But it's okay. Because in that, something very beautiful will happen.

This home is yours.
No mortgage. No loans.

187

If spring came into your life,
would you be prepared?

Are you ready to bloom?

SPRING HAS COME

It's springtime. And the tussle is on. On one side, winter does not want to let go of its hold. On the other side, the warmth of summer wants to break in. This drama is played out in the skies with the clouds, the lightning, the rainbows, and the sun.

On the ground are all these delicate little plants. They're fragile. Last fall, they took a gamble: "Winter will come, and to survive it, we need to shed our leaves." So they did. But the true gamble was not about winter. The true gamble was, "Summer will come again, and when it does, we will be able to put out our leaves and once again become complete."

So now they are ready, and the slightest hint of summer coming has spurred them to start putting new leaves out. And these delicate leaves and delicate flowers are becoming ready to make the commitment to being complete.

YOUR SPRING
If you have observed this, then my question to you is simply this: If spring came into *your* life, would you be prepared? Are you ready to bloom? If you are, I have some very good news for you. Spring has already come. Bloom! This is not the time to reason. This is not the time to question. This is not the time to argue whether spring has come for real or not. It is not the time to lament that once again fall will come and the leaves will have to be shed.

190

Do you know that spring comes into your life every day and that it is vital to be ready? The word is *vital*, not *mandatory*. I'm not saying that if you are not ready, there will be consequences like going to hell or anything like that.

When you think about it, that's what happens with so many religions. A religion, to me, is like a finger pointing toward God. And yet, so many people stop looking where the finger is pointing and concentrate on the finger. And then they say, "My finger is better than your finger. My finger is longer than your finger. My finger is older than your finger. My finger is whiter than your finger." And nobody's looking at where the finger is pointing.

However strong the grip of ignorance is, it will be broken.

The seeker within you is stronger than the sum of all the questions.

Is that what you do in your life? When pain comes, what do you do? What is pain? It's a wake-up call. You know, alarm clocks have obnoxious noises, and there's a reason for that. The point of the alarm clock is to wake you up, not put you back to sleep. If it came on with a harp playing a lullaby, you would relax: "Ahhhh, the alarm has come on. Now I can finally go to sleep." That's not the point of an alarm clock.

YOUR RHYTHM

When pain comes, it's saying, "Hello, haven't we been a little unconscious lately? Awaken. Awaken." But pain comes, and people say, "What is this pain? Let's look at it. Let's analyze it." That's not what pain is for. The grinding of the gears inside happens because something isn't right.

There is a rhythm that you have as a human being. This rhythm says, "Move. March. Go. Understand." Understand your mortality and be inspired to move on. Understand also your *immortality*. Part of you is mortal, and part of you is immortal. You are like a sandwich.

You have paid a lot of attention to one slice of bread, the mortal. You should also pay attention to the other slice, because the mortal will disintegrate. That is its nature. Don't let that scare you. Let it inspire you to focus on the other slice—the immortal—that is really good, truly delicious. Pay attention to the inspiration that resides in your heart. Within you is the drum that plays the beat to know, to move, to dance to its rhythm, to dance the dance of understanding, and to sing, "What a gift I have been given! I understand my urge to blossom."

People say, "I am looking for something, but I don't know what it is."

Remember the gamble that the little plants take to shed their leaves. Without the use of a high-speed Internet connection, satellites, or databases of the years and years of weather data that has been accumulated, they take a certain gamble that isn't really a gamble. Because the beauty is that spring *will* come.

192

THE DRIVE FROM INSIDE

When I look at those tiny bright green leaves emerging, I say to myself, "Go. Move. Don't be threatened. Don't be disheartened because it is cold today. However strong the grip of this cold is, it *will* be broken."

For you, however strong the grip of ignorance is, it will be broken, because the seeker within you is stronger than the sum of all the questions, whatever those questions are, however many millions of questions there are, however much confusion there is in the world. Such is the drive from inside.

This drive to search is the most beautiful drive. And if a person searches, should I be the one to say, "I know what you should be searching for"? No. I say, "You are searching? Good. Search!" Because if you search genuinely, you will find what will help you to fulfill the quest. You *will*.

A lot of people say, "Tell me, how does it happen?" It's called the thirst, the thirsty, and the water. If there was no such thing as thirst, there would be no such thing as the thirsty. But because there is a thirst, there are the thirsty. And because there are the thirsty, water will be found.

The water that you are looking for is within you. That's why it will be found. I'm sure there are people who would think, "Yes, but there are some who die of thirst in the desert." In the desert that I am talking about, all you have to do is remove the sand of ignorance, and the purest, most beautiful, clear water will bubble up, *anywhere*. You don't have to go to a particular place. You don't have to be looking for an oasis, a well, or a river. You don't have to be looking for birds or a clump of trees. You don't have to be looking for anything. You can find the water anywhere in this desert, because the most incredible pump is bringing it up all the time.

Every breath is pumping the most incredible water that will quench your thirst— every breath, day and night. One day, it will not be so. People get surprised by that, and that surprises *me*. Don't be surprised. You *know* this. There are three things: birth, life, and death. Birth has happened, so there's no point in talking about that. The last one is going to happen even if you don't want it to. Life is not about putting coins into a machine and then being able to choose: "Okay, I want this or that. But *that* button I'm never going to push!"

Life is not like that. It's not a gamble. That it will end is certain. To dwell on the end is pointless. Dwell on life. Dwell on the possibility of recognizing that the water is under the sand, the very sand that looks so dry that it discourages you.

Look at the world. Is it not discouraging? I travel to a lot of places talking about peace. But that's not what people are caught up in. They're caught up in things like: "These bank managers made bad decisions." "Two more people were killed." And they are busy trying to justify all the craziness of the world: "Mankind has been fighting throughout history, so this is nothing new." But at the end of each war and each battle, what do people want? Peace.

Look in your heart, and you will find the true essence of your existence. Look within, and you will find the most beautiful waters. Look within, and you will find your solutions. You will find answers to which you don't even have questions.

In the temple of your heart, you will find the holiest of all scriptures that ever will be. A scripture that no one else can read and for which you do not need to know any language. A scripture that is with you day and night. It doesn't threaten you. It doesn't tell you to do things. And most incredible of all, it doesn't need interpretation.

INCREDIBLE ENERGY

Do you need to have faith? Of course you need faith, but in what? I began by saying, "The plants took a gamble." Okay, *gamble* wasn't such a good word. If you think about it, you can actually change that word to *faith*.

Have faith that spring will come. It will come. Be in joy. Understand what you have been given. The greatest of gifts is the coming and going of the breath that you receive.

Do you really want to know if God exists? And when I say "God," I don't mean a god with a face and two eyes and a bad temperament. That's the way many people portray God. I'm talking about the most incredible energy, that doesn't have a face and two eyes but is truly omnipotent, omniscient, and omnipresent; that has passion and compassion; that is holding universes and universes beyond universes together. I'm talking about the energy that puts everything in place, that from dust creates suns, moons, planets.

From nothing, to create everything. To create this earth, to create incredible textures of carpet, ceilings without pillars—alive, beautiful, ever changing. To create a light that is magnificent in every shade. To create night lights that are unimaginable—the moon, the stars, the clouds, all of it. To make a day and never make two alike, to make a moment and never two alike. To make the trees and never two alike, to make a snowflake and never two alike, and to make human beings and never two alike. This is craftsmanship.

And to give you the ability to witness it—not just to see all this but to be able to admire it and say, "How magnificent."

When it pours and pours with rain, remember the magnificence that you have been blessed with. Remember what the possibilities are. Remember that you're part of it. You're not some abstract good-for-nothing who just happened to be. When the

194

craftsmanship is so good, then every bit needs to be looked at and admired. Nothing is frivolous; not a grain of sand is out of place. Not a leaf, a snowflake, or a raindrop is out of place. If you accept that, then you must also accept that *you* are not out of place.

SEE THE REALITY

The ability to admire is one of the human being's greatest achievements. The way you can admire is unique to you. Your gratitude is unique. And it's not out of place. Will your gratitude help God? No. When you feel gratitude, it is *you* who will be touched. When you admire, it is *you* who will be filled with incredible bliss and joy. This is how it is.

You look at your day, and you see your problems. You wonder what will happen to you after you die, but you never wonder what could happen to you while you're alive. You have asked questions, but the wrong ones. Somehow, according to the prevailing pattern, you have a free license to think about heaven and want to be in heaven after you are dead, but you are absolutely not permitted to think about heaven here, now. That concept, to me, is bizarre.

See the reality. Reality is more beautiful than anything you have ever imagined.

Spring comes every day. Accept and gather the opportunity. Be ready to sprout—without hesitation, every day. And once again, be complete. Be whole.

Spring comes every day. Be ready to sprout every day.

And once again, be complete, be whole.

195

ABOUT PREM RAWAT

Prem Rawat has spoken about peace from an early age, inspiring audiences with his unique perspective and wisdom. He speaks from the heart, without script or rehearsal, bringing simplicity to important issues that people often find complex.

Born in India to a prosperous family, Prem Rawat left his native land as a teenager to travel to Europe and America, with a desire to know the world. His driving ideal was to promote an optimistic vision of life and a vision of peace, both individually and collectively. This ideal continues as strongly today, some four decades later.

In pursuit of his life's goal Prem Rawat has maintained a challenging travel schedule since his first international journeys as a young teenager. In an average year, he flies more than 100,000 nautical miles. In 2011 alone he spoke to over 500,000 people at 78 live events worldwide. During that time, there were over 1.1 million downloads of his videos.

Prem Rawat attracts audiences from all walks of life, regardless of education, beliefs, age, or status. As well as speaking before intimate audiences and vast crowds — sometimes, in India, exceeding 300,000 — he has been invited to speak at a number of important institutional venues and forums. These include the European Parliament, the United Nations (UN), the Italian Senate, the parliament buildings of Australia, Argentina and New Zealand, the Young President's Organisation, and the Guildhall in London, as well as numerous universities worldwide.

RECENT ACHIEVEMENTS AND RECOGNITIONS

In November 2011, he was invited as keynote speaker and inspirer of the "Pledge to Peace" launched at the European Parliament, under the patronage of First Vice-President Gianni Pittella. The Pledge to Peace, a call to peaceful action, was the first of its kind ever presented at the European Union, and 37 institutions signed. The pledge activities, announced on UN Peace Day, continue to develop momentum.

In 2012, Prem was awarded the Asia Pacific Brands Association's BrandLaureate Lifetime Achievement award, reserved for statesmen and individuals whose actions and work have positively impacted the lives of people and the world at large. Other recipients of this prestigious award include Nelson Mandela and Hillary Clinton.

In the spring of 2012 he was invited to launch the Third Festival of Peace in Brazil. This initiative, hosted by UNIPAZ (University of International Peace), which works towards world peace, involved more than one million people.

Speaking in a specially prepared video for the Nordic Peace Conference in Oslo, Prem emphasized the very real possibility of peace in our lifetime. He said:

"There are people who are very greedy. There are people who don't care. But in my opinion, that is a minority. The majority of the people on the face of this earth want peace, and if this is true, then peace on earth is a very achievable objective. People say it's not going to happen. Well, let this time belong to those who believe it can happen, not to the ones who say it cannot."

In recognition of his profound impact on individuals and his contribution towards the world's understanding of peace, Prem has received many keys to cities and awards, and has been named an Ambassador of Peace by UNIPAZ and three other governmental organizations.

HUMANITARIAN EFFORTS
In 2001 he established The Prem Rawat Foundation, which addresses the fundamental human needs of food, water, and peace. The Foundation works to make Prem's message of peace widely available throughout the world. Over the past 10 years, the Foundation has provided over 158 grants to aid people in 40 countries across five continents.

Through TPRF, Prem Rawat established the Peace Education Program (PEP), to help people discover their own inner resources. This program is being conducted in over 28 prisons worldwide, and in adult education programs, universities, and a wide variety of other settings. Prem has personally addressed inmates at several prisons around the world. The Peace Education Program is currently the subject of academic study due to its unusually high success rate in reducing recidivism for those incarcerated.

PERSONAL
Prem Rawat embraces creativity and cutting-edge technology. He is an inventor and a highly accomplished pilot, with over 12,000 hours flying time, most of it spent flying himself to his own speaking events. He is married with four adult children.

Made in the USA
Charleston, SC
03 June 2013